THE GOLDEN NIGHTINGALE

THE MACMILLAN COMPANY
NEW YORK · BOSTON · CHICAGO
DALLAS · ATLANTA · SAN FRANCISCO

MACMILLAN AND CO., LIMITED
LONDON · BOMBAY · CALCUTTA
MADRAS · MELBOURNE

**THE MACMILLAN COMPANY
OF CANADA, LIMITED**
TORONTO

THE GOLDEN NIGHTINGALE

Essays on Some Principles of Poetry

in the Lyrics of William Butler Yeats

BY DONALD A. STAUFFER

THE MACMILLAN COMPANY: NEW YORK   1949

"If one writes well and has the patience, somebody will come from among the runners and read what one has written quickly, and go away quickly, and write out as much as he can remember in the language of the highway."

—YEATS, Preface to the third
edition of his *Poems*, 1901.

"To those few people mainly personal friends who have read all that I have written."

—YEATS, Preface to *Reveries over
Childhood and Youth*, 1914.

"Old father, old artificer, stand me now and ever in good stead."

—JOYCE, *A Portrait of the Artist
as a Young Man*.

THIS book has grown out of a series of lectures given at the Johns Hopkins University in April 1948 in the Percy Graeme Turnbull series of memorial lectures. Parts of Chapters II and III have appeared in the *Journal of English Literary History* (September, 1948) and the *Kenyon Review* (Summer, 1949). The author gratefully acknowledges his indebtedness to the above for permission to publish these materials in their present form.

CONTENTS

CHAPTER I *The Search for Truth* I

CHAPTER II *The Medium of Poetry* 24

CHAPTER III *The Reading of a Lyric* 48

CHAPTER IV *The Purpose of Poetry* 80

CHAPTER V *The Progress of a Poet* 108

Notes 129

CHAPTER ONE

THE SEARCH FOR TRUTH

"Wisdom comes of beggary."
—"The Seven Sages."

"But there's another knowledge that my heart destroys,
Because it proves that things both can and cannot be."
—"The Curse of Cromwell."

"I make the truth!"
—*The Death of Cuchulain.*

"Fifteen apparitions have I seen;
The worst a coat upon a coat-hanger."
—"The Apparitions."

SOME men are born poets, some achieve poetry, and some have poetry thrust upon them. Since poetry is no single simple thing, central poetic issues might profitably be considered in the careers of three poets each drawn from one of these classes. The born poet, the original genius warbling his native woodnotes wild, may offer us poetry. So may the dedicated spirit, in his laborious mastery of his art. And so too may the man who has poetry thrust upon him, whether the occasion that creates the poem be the duty of singing as Poet Laureate or the writing of a class ode, the founding of Rome or the death of a favorite cat.

Yet if one man partakes of all three types of poet, he is even a better subject. Who better than William Butler Yeats? He was born a Pre-Raphaelite, with the smell of paint in his nostrils and the sound of poetry in his ears. Through a long life, his unswerving profession was art: if Milton temporarily abandoned poetry to serve as Latin Secretary to the Commonwealth, Yeats temporarily accepted a Senatorship in the Irish Free State to strengthen his poetry and to raise the position of the poet. Basically, the occasion that thrust poetry upon Yeats was the period in which he lived. The great overpopulated century of science and materialism threatened to engulf the imaginative individual, and in rebellion Yeats struck out. Poetry was thrust upon him.[1] *

These essays, therefore, though they consider recurring issues in all poetry—issues to which answers may vary with the poets—concentrate on the convictions, the craftsmanship, and the achievement of a single poet, William Butler Yeats. The questions I should like to ask are four: First, what kind of ideas are best expressed in poetry, and what is the nature and extent of our belief in such poetic ideas? Second, what is the manner of poetic expression? How are ideas, and back of them, beliefs, embodied in a poem? Third, more specifically, what is the nature of a *lyric* poem? How can the lyric attain greatness? And fourth, what is the good of poetry?

Perhaps we are beginning with the hardest question, the relation between poetry and truth, since popularly considered, if a thing is true it is not poetic, and if it is poetic, it is not true. A philosopher like the older and possibly congealing Plato, a man with religious sensitivity like Sir Philip Sidney, a scientist like Sir Francis Bacon—all were at times uneasy in their approach to poetry because it might be, so sweetly and so deceptively and so dangerously, the mother of lies. I have known scientists who felt when young the budding wings of

---

[1] * Notes may be found at the back of the book. The starring of a note indicates that additional material is given to illustrate or explain. All other notes are simple identifications of quotations.

poetry on their shoulders, but who, in the maturity of their late 'teens, put away childish things to devote themselves instead to what they considered accurate knowledge. The question is not lightly to be dismissed: if one believes in first things —God, virtue, truth—will not a passion for poetry warp or diminish them?

Yet let us begin lightly. Let us begin with a small defense of a sense of humor, possibly not important to the argument, since all poets do not notably possess it. At least it exists throughout Yeats. I remember first being attracted toward his poetry because of two qualities: his philosophical force and his humor. How irritating, nevertheless, those two in combination can be! Just when you are about to attain the final answer, the revelation, the stable certainty—suddenly a flash, a quirk, a quip, an irrelevancy, a deliberate vagueness, a calculated incongruity, a guffaw. The ironist must be banished from the republic of discovered truth.

What if certain kinds of truth were not discoverable by mortal men? There are occasions when the loud laugh bespeaks anything but the vacant mind. Yeats uses the weapon of humor whenever he finds that his subject is beyond direct and final statement. And although all poets do not have a sense of humor, most of the best poets possess that quality which is inherent in humor—a sense of man's limitations. I am assuming that man's mental limitations are such that he finds it impossible to state, in terms whose finality is comparable to that of a mathematical equation, the last word about God, for example, or virtue, or truth. If this is granted, then a poet is admirably realistic inasmuch as he does not try to do what he cannot do. Whatever poetry does, it does not state the Newtonian laws of motion—or even the laws of emotion—in Newtonian terms.

When a poet tries for the last word, he usually fails as a poet, and dies into the inanition of rhymed moralizer. His tag lines enter the limbos of the Congressional Record, school readers, and the books of familiar quotations. Longfellow, proclaiming in his "Psalm of Life" that

> Lives of great men all remind us
> We can make our lives sublime,

may generate, or may be seriously trying to generate, moral uplift. But it is not the upsurge of great poetry. It has not the ring of Yeats's short epitaph:

> Draw rein, draw breath.
> Cast a cold eye ·
> On life, on death.
> Horseman, pass by!

The true poets, then, take upon themselves the mystery of things, as if they were God's spies. This does not mean that they seek to be mysterious or incomprehensible; it means that they can never completely forget the mystery. Part of their knowledge, which renders them so trying to rational and dogmatic and prosaic souls, is that the universe does contain a mystery. Yeats was fond of quoting Mallarmé: "A poem is a mystery for which the reader must seek the key." [2] But the key does not lie in the ingenuity of a cross-word puzzle; it lies in the mysteries of life and creation and art and imagination.

Let us go a bit further into this philosophical problem of what the poet knows, or more precisely, of what is the nature of *poetic* knowledge. Among the philosophers, Plato still seems at once the oldest and the newest. In large part his secret lies in the poetic presentation of his ideas. [3] * Much of Aristotle seems archaic because he tried to put all of experience into bounded fields, with separate subdivisions as neat as a real estate development. Many of the other philosophers seem somehow wanting, because they reduce their thought to some absolute pattern: the scholastic logic of Aquinas, the mathematical system of Spinoza, the pure categories of Kant, the biological flux of

Bergson, the wilful limitations imposed upon themselves by Locke and by Dewey, by Marx and by Freud. Often they express the best thought and fashions of their day. But the day ends, and another day dawns, a different time bringing with it a different area of general belief which makes it all but impossible to breathe that earlier fashion of thought.[4] * Yet how can you resist speaking in the current mode?

Perhaps the mode of poetry may free you from the mode of fashion. Plato, or his Socrates, resisted the fashion of the Sophists. The Socratic questioning irony, however, shows clearly enough that one creed cannot successfully be attacked by setting up an opposing creed. Plato remains living because he turned from the *logos*, the final word of truth, to the *mythos*, the story, the fantasy, which suggests truth reverently, and always with the knowledge of man's childlike ignorance before the mysteries. Is it not the method of the parables of Christ? The myth of the cave, the myth of the charioteer and the two horses, Aristophanes' fable on love—this *form* of presenting ideas keeps them perpetually alive and infinitely suggestive. Man's reason, in any historical period, is limited; but who can set limits to man's imaginings, or to their possible effects? Such speculations are above the organized fashions of thought. They cannot be arraigned before a court of current dogma, because the indictment cannot be drawn up. As Sir Philip Sidney says: "The poet never affirmeth. The poet never maketh any circles about your imagination, to conjure you to believe for true what he writes. And therefore, though he recount things not true, yet because he telleth them not for true, he lieth not. . . . Of all writers under the sun the poet is the least liar."

Well then, what *is* the poet's relation to knowledge, if he "telleth things not for true"? A poet is a maker, conscious or unconscious, of hypotheses. Their validity is the same as that for hypotheses in philosophy or politics or physical science. A poet is a skeptic, or a limited mortal, with an unlimited imagination and a vast desire to believe. A poet, as the critics have often noticed, is a creator. In the beginning is his word, which is an act of the imagination. Every poet says, "Let there be light." If he were God, there would be light. He creates hypotheses; [5] * if they are accepted by himself or his readers, to that extent they become realities.

The hypothetical nature of the poet's statement comes out most clearly in philosophical language in a volume by H. Vaihinger, translated as *The Philosophy of 'As if'*. [6] Vaihinger's approach is heuristic, that is, "serving to discover or to stimulate investigation." But it is also practical, since Vaihinger feels that in view of man's limited knowledge, "truth" is simply the most workable error. And it is influenced by recent biological thought in its maintaining that reason is a late-appearing useful biological function: it cannot therefore handle such questions as the origin of the world or of good and evil. Since reason is incompetent, what is man forced to do in order to live with himself and in his world? He must create fictions. Vaihinger distinguishes a fiction from an hypothesis. I have made no such distinction merely because of the emotional contempt which the word "fiction" might stir up in our age of scientific "truth." But Vaihinger thinks of an hypothesis as something which presumably will be proved true. A fiction in his terms is simply a construct to help us get along with our thinking. Fictions may contradict reality or even themselves; they may disappear like scaffolding when their purpose is served; they may be realized consciously as untrue. Yet they are expedient; they work. The subtitle of his book is "A System of the Theoretical, Practical and Religious Fictions of Mankind." We cannot escape fictions; we live by them; they are all-powerful. The worship of the Virgin may give way to eugenics. Ham, Shem, and Japheth may be supplanted by theories of racial inequality. The Fall of Man may be outmoded by utopian dreams of a classless state.

But our fictions we have always with us. This book, *The Philosophy of 'As if'*, should be required reading for absolutists, for those who live in a single climate of thought, for those who hold that truth is obvious, for those who belittle the enormous power of imaginative constructs, and for all poets who would like to know what they are doing.

Children have the right approach to poetry. Say to them "Once upon a time," and they do not demand a by-line, a date, and an Associated Press guarantee. The story is authenticated in proportion to the intensity of its acceptance.[7] * The problem of belief does not consciously come up; and it is far more disturbing and insulting to a child to ask him whether or not he believes in Santa Claus than to tell him categorically that there is no Santa. I raise the problem of belief here only because the rationalists tend to assume that poets are out of their minds, a little above idiots. Actually, poets are simultaneously aware of man's ignorance and his possibilities; while your practical man thinks of neither. When Milton constructed over Chaos a bridge from Hell to the World, he was as aware as you and I of its differences from London Bridge. The poetic state, if we are willing to draw again Coleridge's nice distinction, is not a state of belief; it is a "willing suspension of disbelief."

A mathematician may say: "Let us construct a duodecimal system by substituting 12 for 10." A geometrician may say: "Let us locate points by setting up a system of coordinates with the Y axis at 60 degrees instead of 90 degrees to the X axis." Both systems are possible, and would be as completely descriptive and uniformly consistent as the more conventional systems. Similarly a poet may say: "I shall now speak as if—*als ob* —I were a fallen angel, or myself journeying with Virgil through Purgatory, or a Dane, the son of a dear father murdered." And if the poet works consistently, imaginative intensity will evaporate that initial important assumption of "as if."

This long prologue has been necessary if we are to speak of Yeats's beliefs, for they seem at first glance so fantastic. We are unwilling to accept them as assumptions, as fictions (though Yeats recognized them as such clearly enough), for they do not square with our own. Fortunately, at any rate, he is not neglected in his own day, as Blake and Melville were in theirs. Increasingly he will be understood—by the process of all original poets, who teach new modes of thought through the experience of their own works. Since the process is something like a man pulling himself up by his own bootstraps, a certain time may be needed. Eventually we shall read *The Tower* in preference to "The Lake Isle of Innisfree," and will praise Yeats not because he wrote like other poets but because he wrote like himself.

Our initial consideration is not of his poems, but of the main lines of thought that lie back of them. "Thought" may be the wrong word, for Yeats became a poet, as his father wrote to him, "because you had convictions of the kind that could be best expressed in verse, i.e. convictions that were *desires*, and such as could never be imprisoned in opinions." [8] * One of these convictions or desires was that man must be freed from the shackles of his conventional thought, which in our era has been scientific, pragmatic, and sociological. [9] * He devoted his life, therefore, to anything—to everything—that would break the sterile pattern. He galloped toward the bogies with as much verve as Tam O'Shanter fled from them. No hermetic symbols, no cabalistic doctrine, no extrasensory perceptions, no crystal gazing was too esoteric for William Butler Yeats. If the world accepted Darwin and Marx and Dewey, then Yeats would take Plotinus and Swedenborg and Jacob Boehme. He would converse with the superstitious Irish folk and look through the collarbone of a hare. He would conduct long conversations by telepathy with his uncle and their Irish maid. He would disregard Trotzsky and accept Madame Blavatsky. He would hail the superhuman and summon up the great hosts of the Sidhe to ride on the slopes of his own Ben Bulben. A medium to him was no golden mean, but a golden extreme to balance the extreme of science. A spiritualistic séance was more noteworthy than a sitting of Parliament, simply because too many people thought the opposite. To cure a poisoned world, he offers excessive and amazing antitoxins. And if anyone takes his lifelong interest in the occult as a series of Irish whims, failing to see the underlying fighting philosophic principle, then the critic is the one to be laughed at, not Yeats.

"Anything connected with the life of the spirit," says Mary Colum of her friend,[10] "or the emotions or the beliefs of mankind—anything, no matter how farfetched, that human intellect or even superstition had ever owed allegiance to—stirred up an eager movement in his mind."

Yeats has been accused of being a *poseur*. But his poses were deliberately assumed, assumed not *pour épater les bourgeois*, but to teach them. The long cape, the flowing tie, the brown velveteen jacket, the cawing voice, the chanted poetry, were no mere affectations, but a declaration of every man's right to be himself, to *act himself out*. Yeats consciously assumed a Mask— the word is his own—and wore it until it became part of himself, an antithetical part, according to his own philosophy.[11] * Since he believed he was naturally shy and timid, he would flaunt himself boldly; he would create the great reckless figure, in his life as well as in his poetry. He acted out Milton's sentence, that he who would write well "ought himself to be a true poem."

We are verging close upon the formal statement of a philosophy in Yeats's book *A Vision*. And we might as well make the plunge into that coruscating and unique work.

To enter the world of *A Vision* is much more than a journey through the looking glass. It is like going through a kaleidoscope and emerging in a world of Euclidean geometric shapes which interlock and gyrate like Ferris wheels, perpetual-motion machines, and merry-go-rounds in some fantastic amusement park. A human life, this Irishman suggests, may be compared to spirals traced on two transparent cones so related that the tip of each cone touches the center of the base of the other, and as one spiral narrows, the other expands. Or it may be compared to a watch face with four hands and twenty-eight numbers on the dial; two hands are always diametrically opposite the other two; while also in another movement, the two sets of hands move counter to each other, balancing their positions in the spatial pattern, as if they were reflected in a mirror set vertically in the watch face. The cones and the clock faces and the souls are always moving, in opposition and in patterned repetition and in the sequences of a fugue, and in recurrences of threes, fours, and sevens. And the four hands of the clock are the parts of the soul: the Creative Mind (which might be called the Imaginative Intellect) and its opposite, the Body of Fate (which corresponds roughly to external circumstance); the Will (which is the person as he is) and its opposite, the Mask (which is the person as he would like to be, his ideal life). There are 28 numbers or places on the dial because there are 28 phases of the moon; and in the transmigration of souls, your Will may spring up in any of these positions, which will dictate the patterned positions of your Mask, your Creative Mind, and your Body of Fate.

Yet what I have called the Clock Face which governs the individual soul in its many incarnations is also a diagram for the phases of the moon in its waxing and waning. And if one thinks of general history, history waxes and wanes as it goes through the cycle of the Great Wheel. To fulfill this cycle requires a little over two thousand years, although here too there are two great cones with interlocking gyres, so that as one spiral waxes the other wanes. This historical cycle on the Great Wheel is only one of twelve cycles that fulfills a greater movement of 26,000 years (corresponding to Plato's Golden Year) which must elapse before the planets are again in their places, reproducing an original pattern and allowing another cosmic dance to begin.

Yeats finds a place for the individual in this overpowering dance of the stars, this vast *pavane* where the metronome ticks millenniums. He has geared wrist watches into cosmic machinery. The pattern is formidable and formal; all is held in place by ceremony and return, by powerful oppositions of full moon and dark moon, antithetical and primary, subjective and objective, beauty and flux, intellect and body, man and world. It requires a strong visual imagination to sense the rigidly balanced and simultaneous motions of cones and wheels and changing moons. How should one visualize, for instance, though its philosophical importance is easy to realize, the following added complication? Outside the twelve two-thousand-year cycles that make the Great Cycle is the Thirteenth Cone, or Sphere, or Cycle, which provides an escape from the shackling mechanism of Yeats the great watchmaker.[12] *

The reader cannot be expected to grasp this summary of *A Vision*. In fact, it would take many hours of close application to see how inadequate is this outline of the structure itself, entirely apart from its significance. Yeats spent almost twenty years on its creation, and admits that parts of it he does not fully understand. In such collapsing of the mechanism into a dozen or so sentences, I have done great injustice to the ingenuity of Yeats's subtle mind, a bobbin "where all time is bound and wound," [13] turning in upon itself for two decades.

I intended to do further injustice, this time to scholarship, by refusing at this point to consider parallels and sources. I shall not argue about Plato and Spengler, nor horoscopes and astrology. And I shall not build up a case for Yeats's astonishingly wide reading by mentioning his casual references.[14] *

I have presented a few bare bones of this extraordinary system merely to emphasize the question: "What in all this does Yeats *believe*?" Are we to take seriously this whirling geometrical phantasm? This perilous construct, this wilfully rigid mechanism—surely this is the spider spinning gossamer out of his own bowels, and surely we must return to the bee for sweetness and light!

Let us not abandon the spider before we look at some strands in his web, and follow along a little the thread Yeats himself spins in talking of the grounds for his belief or knowledge. Above all, let us try not to do him the violence of reading him on a single plane. Yeats himself speaks with some contempt of "violent men, each master of some generalization." [15] We have been living, he thinks, in this period of intellectual violence, now intensifying itself, during which "Men change rapidly from deduction to deduction, opinion to opinion, have but one impression at a time and utter it always, no matter how often they change, with the same emphasis." [16] A man who can speak so eloquently of the danger of dogmatism is not apt to fall into it himself. Even within the actual context of *A Vision*, Yeats becomes tentative whenever he introduces the question: *How* and *what* do I know? "May I not use such tales?" [17] he will ask. He poses a question where his system makes possible an assertion, yet he answers with no more than a "Perhaps." [18] He compares his symmetrical Great Wheel with Plato's, yet immediately adds: "Plato may have brought such an ideal year into the story, its periods all of exactly the same length, to remind us that he dealt in myth." [19] And no one is in peril of being taken in by his own imaginings who can write: "When I relate this symbol to reality various fancies pass before the mind." [20] *

All of these instances of self-awareness occur in the system itself. Even more interesting in our quest is the framework, the succession of Chinese boxes he builds around the central

vision. In its first form, Yeats tells us, the system was intro-
duced by concocting the figure of Michael Robartes, who brings
back from his Eastern travels a book called *Speculum Ange-
lorum et Hominum*. Edmund Dulac's portrait of Giraldus, the
author of this book (which was "printed at Cracow in 1594"),
looks remarkably like William Butler Yeats in a turban and
beard; and the whole seems a high-spirited hoax. Its credibility
appears about on a par with Virginia Woolf's *Orlando*, and
considerably less than Gertrude Stein's *Autobiography of Alice
B. Toklas*. But in another place,[21] Yeats says he invented the
Robartes framework in order to conceal the genuine source of
his material, which he calls "an incredible experience." [22] In
its final form, Yeats frames *A Vision* by giving the actual history of its origins.

On October 24, 1917, four days after his marriage, his wife,
who had mediumistic tendencies, surprised Yeats by attempting
automatic writing. For nearly two years, the raw material for
A Vision was set down in automatic writing by his wife, who
was fatigued by her almost daily task, and who seemed ignorant
of its meaning and not so wildly excited as her husband in
understanding it. Then, from 1919 until 1920, when these
strange visitations came to an end, she spoke in a trance or a
sleep, and Yeats recorded these strange words which were not
her own, the voices of his teachers who "did not seem to speak
out of her sleep but as if from above it, as though it were a
tide upon which they floated." [23] From these years of writing
and speaking and of his own questioning, Yeats developed by
inference the nature of these visitants, the lightning quickness
of their thought, their ignorance of physical conditions in this
world, the qualities and limits of their knowledge, the questions
which were needed to stimulate their thinking, the shiftings
and fadings, the ingenious and sometimes cruel Frustrators that
made the automatic script or the spectral voices deteriorate
into sentiment or confusion. Once an Instructor, or Com-

municator—or was it a Frustrator?—said: "Remember we will deceive you if we can." [24]

What was the result? One might expect that it would be comparable to reading a ghostly letter written in invisible ink by the light of will-o'-the-wisps and marsh fires. But by 1920, its physical bulk is weighty enough: some fifty copybooks of automatic script, and a much smaller number of books recording what had come in sleep.[25] Over this Yeats worked with passion and despair, with excitement and brooding, until in 1936 he put by his final version which yet did not satisfy him. The first version (as he describes it in 1928 or later) filled him with shame, because he misunderstood the geometry and the philosophical "distinctions upon which the coherence of the whole depended." [26]

Yet one can hardly misunderstand something without believing that there is something there to understand. What was Yeats trying to understand, and in what sense did he take it? Was the Great Mind and the Great Memory as he calls it elsewhere in his prose, the *Anima Mundi* as he calls it in his poetry, trying to speak to him? Or were this script and these voices merely odd manifestations of his own thought? [27] * Or were the "communicators" disembodied persons? Here, too, his answers are multivalent. He had proof, he says,[28] that the communicators were not dependent on his wife's memory or his own; nevertheless, they used modes of expression which Yeats had already used in *Per Amica Silentia Lunae*,[29] and he read over all that his wife had read in philosophy, seeking a possible clue for their symbolic geometry. He recorded that the mysterious agents repeatedly insisted "that the whole system is the creation of my wife's Daimon and of mine, and that it is as startling to them as to us." [30]

To put it with extreme restraint, it startles the reader, too. Is it not possible that Yeats intends to shock and startle the reader toward some new belief, some new way of looking at the world? A period of madness or fantasy is almost the necessary plowing up before new beliefs are possible. *The Waste Land* and *King Lear* tell us that much. Yeats is cunning in his devices. He uses realism and describes in detail the smells of roses and burning feathers that accompany the manifestations. It is somewhat startling to learn that these otherworldly voices first spoke through Mrs. Yeats in a sleeping compartment in southern California. He will startle us with imaginations casually tossed off,[31] * as when we learn that Michael Robartes was meditating on the fascinating spatial hypothesis that the universe is a great egg that turns inside-out perpetually without breaking its shell.[32] And when we begin to take him with too painful a seriousness, he startles us with humor in the grand manner: "Then comes the famous sentence: 'As for living, our servants will do that for us'. I was wondering what made them do anything so absurd." [33] Or: "I knew that the longest life could do but little, and wishing especially to benefit those who lacked what I possessed, I decided to devote my life to the cuckoos." [34] He startles us by defending his rigid system as the only means of presenting the most tenuous thought: "Some, perhaps all, of those readers I most value, those who have read me many years, will be repelled by what must seem an arbitrary, harsh, difficult symbolism. Yet such has almost always accompanied expression that unites the sleeping and waking mind." [35] *

He startles us by suddenly pulling the props out from under the entire artifice with an epilogue in which he drops the mask and allows us to glimpse, with almost painful directness, a creator at work: "Day after day I have sat in my chair turning a symbol over in my mind, exploring all its details, defining and again defining its elements, testing my convictions and those of others by its unity, attempting to substitute particulars for an abstraction like that of algebra. I have felt the convictions of a lifetime melt though at an age when the mind should be rigid, and others take their place, and these in turn give way to others." [36] The insistence of the crowd and of the present breaks in upon his meditations and he asks, as if an inquiring reporter had posed the question: "How far can I accept social- istic or communistic prophecies?" He answers as the poet who creates images normally answers direct queries. He substitutes a quartette of particulars for the abstract reply, bringing out with irony the bitter gap between man's hopes and his estate— Balzac's Duchesse de Castries, William Morris's supper-table, the Japanese saint and labor leader Kagawa, a Communist plow- man on the Cotswold Hills. But these are fractured atoms whirled beyond the circuit of the shuddering Bear, and he rounds off the tragic paragraph with this return: "Then I draw myself up into the symbol and it seems as if I should know all if I could but banish such memories and find everything in the symbol."

The most tragic words in *A Vision* then follow (he is writ- ing between 1934 and 1936): "But nothing comes—though this moment was to reward me for all my toil."

A Vision, then, is a unique passionate book.[37] * A poet is constructing a system, and this in itself would seem a violent attempt to yoke the two incompatibles of mystery and science. Yeats's technique is remarkable. He insists upon shattering our comfortable habits of thought by all the devices he can con- jure up: by huge strange geometrical systems, by paradoxically fantastic tales, by intractable ghostly intruders set off against the circumstantial details in the domestic life of Mr. and Mrs. Yeats, by subtle and original bits of literary criticism expressed in the odd language of the formal system, by casual psycho- logical studies of anyone and everyone seen against the pattern of eternity. Here, surely, is a metaphysician who sees the macrocosmos and the microcosmos in terms of each other, as clearly as did John Donne, whom Yeats resembles also in the power and passion of his thought. If we are looking, in any deep sense, for a metaphysical poet, of all those writing in English since the seventeenth century Yeats (with the possible exception of Eliot) is the most likely candidate.

In his system Yeats has given us a brilliant series of fictions, innumerable bold sallies into the region of "As if," that confident jugglery with hypotheses which shows his complete awareness of the way in which the artist lives with knowledge. The knowledge of the poet is presentational, not argumentative; it lives in pictures, not abstractions; it is tied to particulars as inextricably as experience itself; and if it expresses ideas, those ideas will include the mysteries, the uncertainties, and the hopes which have made most men through most ages know that free will is a fact. The knowledge of the poet is not single, but multiple; he lives in a world of choice, not of cold, hard, unchanging determinism.

One of the embarrassing necessities of criticism is that it must simplify those literary materials which by their very nature are falsified by simplification. I hope that this long prelude indicates my awareness of the murder I am about to commit in order to dissect. It remains justified only as long as we realize that the fundamental answers in all their complexity remain open to inquirers, and amenable to the new needs of new times, in Yeats's complete work.

And with this warning, I shall now proceed happily to a simple listing of some of the main beliefs that find various expressions in Yeats's thought. To put it in a sentence which, as Yeats expands it, has terrific reverberations, Yeats believed in courage, aristocracy, desire, individuality, custom and ceremony, wholeness through oppositions, and immortality. In such extreme form, his beliefs are ridiculously oversimplified.[38] * To give them their full flesh and intertissues, it would be necessary to read all of his works—for none is irrelevant—with a running commentary. We must here strike a workable balance and

expand each one slightly but without quotation, hoping that
the succeeding chapters may bring back into his poetry these
bare bones of belief.

Yeats believed in <u>courage</u>. His commitment to life was as
unequivocal as it can ever be in a poet. There was no room
in his living for world-weariness, and everyone has noted the
miraculously increasing youth and vigor of his writings as he
grew older. It is as if life for him were a heady drink, and long
quaffing could only increase the frenzy and the Dionysian
affirmation. He could understand, and in a way share, the savage views of Nietzsche and of Swift, since the strength of their
denials is but another manifestation of vitality. But though he
could write from intimate experience of "the Tragic Generation," the frail ineffectuals of the nineties, yet the delicate
pastel shades of their despair were not to be his, nor was their
tragedy. Homer was his example, and his unchristened heart.
Out of the strong shall come forth sweetness, as the honeycomb from the lion's carcass in Samson's riddle. His acceptance
of life, however, did not prettify it. What theme had Homer
but original sin? Rage and lust and love's bitter mysteries are
parts of life and themes for poetry. He did not embrace life
by imagining it as a Utopia, existent or about to be; nor did
he become a great lover of little things such as white plates and
cups or the cool kindliness of sheets.[39] * No: if we are looking
for a parallel, his courage is the courage of Beethoven.

Courage, if it is precious, is also rare. It is the gift of the few,
the leaders, the prophets, the heroes. Yeats is no democrat.
The common people cannot be helped by making them comfortable in their commonness. Yeats is an <u>aristocrat</u> because of
his admiration for those high qualities that are the possession
of a few.[40] * His aristocracy is not one of privilege but of pain
—of strenuous spiritual achievement. There will be no compromise with the narrowness and blindness and fanaticism of
Paddy and the vulgar many; no blurring of values. And since

to him values are all-important and come in hierarchies, Yeats is an aristocrat in his beliefs.

Yet the more vital the value, the harder it is to achieve. The common man who sits in his house by the side of the road is horrifyingly dead in his complacency. He is a half-man, if that. Desire—impossible desire—is the sign of life.[41] * Though it may be but a small straw in the wind, it is significant that "The Lake Isle of Innisfree" was inspired not by a beautiful island but by the streets of London. The movement of Yeats's thought is always "I will arise and go now," and not "I have arrived." *A Vision* is shot through with the tensions and tractions of desire. There is the great Blakean mythological figure of Yeats's archer shooting the arrow of desire out of this flat plane of time and space.[42] * There is the pull of the Will toward the Mask—that diametrically opposed and impossible ideal that directs each individual. There is the pull exerted by the circumstances of our mortal lot, our Body of Fate, diametrically upon our Creative Mind. And there is the groping and searching of Creative Mind toward Mask, or of Will toward Body of Fate. In its simplest terms, Yeats sees life as desire.

Without going into the complexities of the cones and the clock face, without literally calculating the mathematical permutations possible among the planetary pulls of so many facets of the human spirit and human experience, we may say that multiple desires make possible an almost infinite variety of human beings. Yeats believes in human individuality; he feels a horror toward the abstract, a world which he uses almost as a fetish of revulsion against the inhuman. The "mire and blood," those repeated symbols that show so well Yeats's vitalism, are the stuff of human life; and in strange patterns of desire for each, the "fury and the mire of human veins" give us our individuality as persons. Yeats is the great champion of the individual in a century in which great social and scientific and economic forces are tending to crush him like elephants treading upon an ant. Even while Yeats is in process of setting up his system, he cannot refrain from including the most delicate and novel psychographs of such people as Carlyle, Blake, Shelley, Synge, Lady Gregory, and Shakespeare, which show his sensitivity to the subtleties of human character and the independence of the human spirit.

Yet also the great pattern persists, and these individuals, glowing for a moment on the wheel of time, play their part in the great dance.[43] * The "fury and the mire of human veins" flow through us all, but did not begin with our births as individuals, nor shall cease at our deaths. In a triple creed almost as famous as Eliot's avowal of classicism, Anglicanism, and royalism, Yeats sets up as two of his beliefs the belief in the Great Mind and in the Great Memory.[44] I think this accounts in part for the odd fact that in spite of his poses, his masks, and his passionate belief in the individual, Yeats does not strike us as being an egotist. [45] * Each of us is but a small part of the whole, even the leaders taking their places in the great design. The Great Mind and the Great Memory explain his toying with the ideas of reincarnation and metempsychosis. His theory of history is cyclical; when a phase of living swings round again, men may be born who resemble their forebears without losing their individuality. These are the forms of expression—the song of Pythagoras, the Great Wheel, the Great Mind, the Great Memory—which Yeats chooses to give to his reverence for custom and ceremony.[46] * "Before the world began" Yeats made a bargain with the cosmic pattern. It is ironical that this man, whose thought seems to many so original and strange and perverse that they distrust it, uses as two of his most heavily charged words "custom" and "ceremony."

But we have not begun to plumb the secrets of Yeats's thought until we accept such antitheses and paradoxes. Each of his ideas thrives upon its antinomy, and indeed cannot be understood without it. He is an unconscious Manichean and a

dualist. To him the condition of full human existence presupposes an awareness of contradictions.[47] * Desire reaches
across the world. Opposites exert fated attractions. Man yearns
for wholeness, but the state of wholeness he can never reach
as man; pure matter or pure spirit are inhuman. Our state as
mortals, therefore, should be to desire that wholeness while
comprehending in ourselves the oppositions and contradictions
that make it impossible.

It is this comprehension, this steadily felt and never satisfied
desire for wholeness, which constitutes in one sense Yeats's
belief in immortality. He is certain, as are most great artists,
of the permanence of art. But it is more than that. It is the
permanence, or the recurrence, of significant life. He has taken
Browning's idea of

> There shall never be one lost good! What was, shall
>   live as before;

and has given it salient dignity in an imaginative cosmology of
all history and all spirit. He has trafficked with strange mer-
chants; like Doctor Faustus he has invaded the regions of the
dead, has touched upon necromancy and magic, has walked in
forbidden precincts and breathed dizzying airs. And he has
reached a conviction of immortality—not so much of personal immortality as of the recurrence of the pattern in a
permanent cyclical life-force, the persistence of the passionate
moments of the spirit, the sense of our minds and memories
flowing into one another and thereby conquering the desperate
phantoms of Time with his hourglass and Death with his sickle.

The conviction of immortality, which I have described so
inadequately, protects him from the sin of pride, for the individual is of value almost in proportion to his awareness of himself as a part of greater designs. Yeats's aristocratic hierarchy
of spiritual values is too austere to permit shallow personal
vanities. The dignity and worth of the individual is preserved

precisely because of his larger significance, cosmic, traditional, ceremonial. At the same time Yeats is protected from the sin of despair, since his cyclical theory of history saves him from hopeless drifting, and from the idea of constant retrogression and decadence, and equally from a shallow or rationalistic belief in progress which the hard realities of existence can so dangerously and speedily turn into desperation. His belief in antitheses and antinomies protects him from one-sided idealisms or fanaticisms, for opposites are necessary to the establishment of any value; and in Yeats, like desires unlike.[48] *

This chapter must close by a return to a consideration of courage. Yeats's beliefs are self-made, more than those of any other important poet since Wordsworth. His was a long life of introspection.[49] * Though in his later career he read widely enough to be surprised at the parallels and correspondences between his own thought and that of others, his thought remains his own. It was proved upon his pulses; or better, it was distilled from his own passion, his own blood. He cannot accept Christianity, because Christianity cannot fully accept the world. He is not satisfied with any creed, nor will he set up a creed of his own for followers, since the belief in desire is a perpetual becoming and change, and the belief in oppositions destroys any single certainty. Instead, he translates his beliefs into action, and lives out the life of the rebel, the lonely antagonist of destiny, in order to keep us from the comfortable acceptance of our one world of abstraction, whether it be called science, or pragmatism, or materialism, or economic socialism, or progress, or the century of the common man.

It is a hard road, the road of the chameleon who continually changes his color, when the world is crying for a permanent black and a permanent white. But it is one road of the artist, perhaps the typical road. It is the road of images, of speculations, of *mimesis*, of *mythos*. It proceeds by a constant throwing out of alternatives and hypotheses that keep us alive to the

possibilities of choosing.[50] * The world we live in is constructed
on a multitude of "As if"s, big and little, and the imaginative
artist is the man most fully aware of them. He is therefore the
man who most nearly approaches reality.[51] * Pieter Breughel
has a satiric painting of blind beggars leading blind beggars.
Although Yeats is not so intransigent in agnosticism as Breughel, he too is aware of man's limitations. A sound knowledge,
as Socrates knew long ago, is based upon a knowledge of self
and a confession of one's blindness and ignorance. But it is
based also upon knowledge of one's possibilities.

In the search for truth, the poet proceeds into mystery. He
is endowed with hope and with love. In creating possibilities,
in inventing a world which may be, or many worlds which
may be, he sets forth his faith, his belief. And his search for
truth presents, finally, the most faithful description we have
of the human condition: our consciousness accepting the particulars of the world, surrounded by mysteries, and given form
and direction by an act of the mind in the creation of infinite
possibilities.

CHAPTER TWO

THE MEDIUM OF POETRY

"I must leave my myths and symbols to explain themselves
as the years go by and one poem lights up another."
—*Poems*, 1912, p. xi.
Preface to 3d ed., 1901.

A POEM presupposes a belief of some sort.[1] * Any form of
expression, for that matter, would seem to indicate enough
belief in something to rouse the desire to express and to com-
municate. But belief is not sufficient to produce a good poem,
even if that belief is of a poetic nature—even if that belief is
imaginatively aware of many ways of saying "Perhaps," emo-
tionally aware of human life, and sensuously aware of the
world about us. A poem is a made thing, just as much as a
willow whistle or a steamship. It cannot carry on its life without help from the world outside the artist's mind. If a poem
is to result, therefore, technical skill must be added to inner
conviction. A belief in home will not produce a house; neither
will a belief in God-in-nature produce "Tintern Abbey."

When we consider the technique of poetry, immediately we
are confronted by one of the paradoxes of art: how can form
be given to the formless? If a poem is a made thing, to be apprehended through eye and ear, how can it carry such intangibles as, say, Yeats's admiration of courage or ceremony?
In terms of poetry, the question revives the old puzzle of the

relation of the body and the soul. We cannot define the soul of poetry any more than we can define the soul of man. But each of us, if we have ever experienced a poem, has intimations that poetry develops out of (and at the same time includes) intuitions and speculations, hopes and prayers, desires so strong that they seem burning ideals or flaming indignations. Of such disembodied moods and emotions the soul of poetry may be composed.

It is extremely difficult, however, to imagine even for a short moment this distinct soul of poetry, this *élan vital* that calls it into being. For unless we ourselves are creating poets, we experience a poem as something already created. It has already taken on a body; and once it becomes a living poem, not even the scalpel of the critic can cut out from it that quality that brought it into being. An easier task is to consider the body of the poem itself, for certainly one may say specific and formal things about a concrete form. We can all see that a poem is composed of ordered words. We can, then, scrutinize the words, the diction. We may also look at the order: at that particular ordering of words in poetry that we call rhythm; or at the order which comes from placing, sequence, inversion, relationship; or at the symmetry of the parts, in lines, stanzas, and sections; or at the form gained through infinitely various applications of the idea of repetition. We may consider the imagery in details as small as an adjective or as large as the structure of the story or the created illusion of its actors; and we may play with the contrasts and oppositions, the dominant proportions, that give structure to the whole.

Simultaneously in these two parts, then—soul and body—a poem exists. Impulse is given form. The boundless assumes an outline. A poem might be defined as a formal *presentation* of emotion or of interpreted experience. It might be defined as the *envisioning* of values, as its title often suggests—The *Masque* of Mercy, The *House* of Life. Always, if the two needful aspects are remembered, the paradox of poetry is present, and the boundless is given a boundary.

To express it in another image, the work of art lives at the point where the two cones of an hourglass meet. The sand runs through. In which direction is the sand running? As we experience the poem, is it the intangibles taking on shape and form? Or is it the succession of bright images, sharp words, beautiful forms, turning themselves, as they enter that other cone, into emotions and aspirations? It is both: an *experienced* work of art is indivisible.

More consciously, perhaps, than any poet who has ever written in English, William Butler Yeats was preoccupied with this technique of preserving the essential indivisibility of a poem. Since criticism implies distinguishing, separating, dividing, we must realize at the start that the only justification for the analysis of Yeats's method lies in the hope that we may return to his poems *as wholes* with clearer appreciation. We must introduce for a time that poetic evil of abstraction in order to see how the poet escapes from it altogether.

Yeats makes a distinction between symbolism and allegory, which, in one of its forms, might here be quoted not so much to define the two terms satisfactorily, as to show the bent of Yeats's mind toward unity in art. "A symbol," he says, "is indeed the only possible expression of some invisible essence, a transparent lamp about a spiritual flame; while allegory is one of many possible representations of an embodied thing, or familiar principle, and belongs to fancy and not to imagination: the one is a revelation, the other an amusement." [2] *

This conception of the symbol as "the only possible expression of some invisible essence" makes it extremely difficult to talk about symbols at all. In the first place, who is to determine that the symbol is the *only* possible expression? The poet himself? If so, we fall rapidly into the personal and private heresies of the French symbolists and of many modern poets, who construct puzzles from their unique experiences which only an omniscient God can unriddle. Take Yeats's poem called "The Second Coming." If we hold rigidly to the notion that only the poet's full mental experience can give the adequate symbol for the idea the title suggests, then we must not call up some conventional painting of Christ in a glory. No; we must pronounce the words "The Second Coming!" and follow precisely Yeats's own experience when he writes: "I began to imagine, as always at my left side just out of the range of the sight, a brazen winged beast that I associated with laughing, ecstatic destruction." [3]

Can a poem evoke such personal symbols complete and precise? In Yeats's poem, the beast is there, but no one would know offhand that it had wings, was brazen, or was on our left side just out of sight. Although there are many personal symbols in Yeats's poems, undoubtedly vivid to him but not transferable to most of his readers, long experience taught Yeats to avoid this type of idiosyncrasy. His typical poems are not based on unreinforced personal symbols; the best of them need not float upon a bottomless quagmire of annotation.

A second difficulty is this: if a symbol is the only possible expression of some invisible essence, how can we analyze it at all? Are we not confronted with the dilemma of all mystics, who cannot describe their mystical experience because if it were describable it would not be unified but composite? How then is a unique experience transferable? A start toward a solution lies in Yeats's belief in the Great Mind and the Great Memory [4] *—that the thoughts of any mind, those of the dead as well as of the living, are not bounded by personality, but may flow into other minds. If we do not wish to accept this belief in Yeats's terms, common sense will at least allow that there is such a thing as *common* sense, and that men possess experience that may be shared.

But the essence of Yeats's solution is to be found in his conception of the unifying imagination. In his theory of art, as elsewhere, Yeats may be considered one of the latest of the Romantics. He is of the tribe of Wordsworth and Coleridge, Blake and Shelley. Allegory, he has said, is an amusement of the fancy, making almost the Lake Poets' distinction, which is more a judgment of value than of kinds. Fancy for Yeats is the superficial play of intellect, which, desiring to embody Courage, will choose among a lion, a mother bird, Saint Sebastian, and Horatius at the bridge. One is as good as another; none is inevitable. But symbolism is revelation; it is "the only possible expression"; it belongs to imagination in Coleridge's sense of the harmonious indivisible complete functioning of the poet's mind.

"I am now certain," Yeats writes, "that the imagination has some way of lighting on the truth that the reason has not." [5] What are the characteristics of these imaginative poetic symbols?

1. Each is unified and indivisible.

2. Each has a meaning—since Yeats is no theorist of "pure poetry," content to rest in the ineffable name.

3. Though a symbol is as indivisible as a perfect sphere, one may view its hemispheres, seeing the permanent expressed in the particular, the dreaming in the waking, the boundless in the bounded.

4. This complex meaning is untranslatable; it cannot satisfactorily be expressed in other terms.

5. Each symbol is inexhaustibly suggestive, rooted in the past, whether the past is that of the artist or of mankind.

6. Each symbol has a moral meaning, in the wide sense that a sympathetic awareness of reality makes men better.

7. Each symbol is self-creating, and cannot be deliberately sought.

8. Each symbol grows slowly, its existence often realized before its meaning is understood.

9. Every artist has his central symbol, or a group of related symbols that form a dominating symbolic pattern.

10. And finally, this unified symbol constitutes a revelation.

This, then, is Yeats's decalogue on symbolism, consistently expressed throughout his writings and exemplified in his poems. His own words may give body and beauty to these related propositions, with reinforcements and echoes in the notes. A poetic symbol is unified, meaningful, complex, untranslatable, inexhaustibly suggestive, moral, self-creating, slow-growing, centrally important, and revelatory.

The idea of unity is the beginning and end of this conception of symbolism, no matter what digressions we may make on the journey. Yeats is as convinced as Benedetto Croce that intuition and expression are one, and indeed the two of them find common support in the English Romantics. Yeats quotes with approval Blake's sentence: "I am, like others, just equal in invention and execution." And again: "No man can improve an original invention; nor can an original invention exist without execution, organized, delineated and articulated either by God or man." 6 *

Blake's remarks, however, consider technique as an inevitably perfect mirror of inspiration. Usually Yeats stresses instead the Coleridgean unity-of-the-imagination that makes it impossible to distinguish the various *faculties* of the human spirit. A symbol is a kind of supernatural embodiment, so that Yeats may say:

"It is still true that the Deity gives us . . . His flesh and blood, and I believe that the elaborate technique of the arts, seeming to create out of itself a superhuman life, has taught more men to die than oratory or the Prayer Book. We only believe in those thoughts which have been conceived not in the brain but in the whole body." 7 * He states flatly that "It is not possible to separate an emotion or a spiritual state from the image that calls it up and gives it expression." 8 His beautiful image for the unifying symbol is that of the fountain: "Art bids us touch and taste and hear and see the world, and shrinks from what Blake calls mathematic form, from every abstract thing, from all that is of the brain only, from all that is not a fountain jetting from the entire hopes, memories, and sensations of the body." [9] This unifying symbol can guide races and inspire individuals.[10] *

Such a power as the symbol, as Yeats conceives it, must have meaning. This would hardly need stating if there were not those who mistakenly believe that because symbolism transcends reason, symbolism must be meaningless. In repeated implication, Yeats makes his position on this point so clear that a single direct statement from his vigorous philosophical mind is sufficient here. He quotes Goethe with approval: "A poet needs all philosophy, but he must keep it out of his work." Yeats goes further and immediately adds: "though that is not always necessary." [11] Far from advocating *la poésie pure*, therefore, Yeats suggests that it is occasionally possible to have *la philosophie pure* as part of a genuine poetic creation.[12] *

Ordinarily, the symbol presents a double world: "some invisible essence" in its embodiment. These two aspects, though bound "like the yoke and white of the one shell," [13] Yeats can at least talk of in prose. "True art is expressive and symbolic," he writes, "and makes every form, every sound, every colour, every gesture, a signature of some unanalyzable imaginative essence." [14] Our every-day life is troubled by the breath from these invisible essences, like the trembling of a veil, like the bending of reeds when the wind is among them.[15] * Art is created where the two modes of being meet—the unearthly glory and the light of common day. Again and again Yeats returns to his conception of the trancelike state, between sleeping and walking, where the timeless, for a moment, enters into the world of time.[16] * An essence becomes a presence. This marriage of two modes of being, which Yeats traces back into his own flesh-and-blood ancestry,[17] * is the poet's need. To Yeats it is so sacred that almost in the spirit of Wordsworth's "Intimations," he obscures the distinction between the bounded and the boundless, that each may partake of the other: "I am orthodox and pray for a resurrection of the body, and am certain that a man should find his Holy Land where he first crept upon the floor, and that familiar woods and rivers should fade into symbol with so gradual a change that he never discover, no, not even in ecstasy itself, that he is beyond space, and that time alone keeps him from Primum Mobile, Supernal Eden, Yellow Rose over all." [18]

Such a sentence as the last, richly symbolic in itself, suggests the great weight of meaning that Yeats attaches to symbols. Rooted in tradition, trancelike, inexhaustible—how obvious it should be that the symbol cannot be translated into common terms, or survive the ordeal of discursive reason! An allegory, being a rational equation, may be expressed in various other forms, just as we can say with equal truth that two is either one plus one, or the square root of four. But a symbol cannot be expressed in any other terms. The expression is the symbol: change the expression, try to extract an equivalent meaning in some other mode, and the symbol dies. This truth seems less esoteric and stubbornly mysterious to the man on the street, when he considers Yeats's answer to one of those well-meaning and serious amateurs who hound poets with the question: "Is this paraphrase what you *really* mean? Is this what you were trying to say?" Yeats's answer: "I don't want to interpret the 'Death of the Hare.' . . . If an author interprets a poem of his own he limits its suggestibility. *You* can say that the poem means that . . . etc." [19] This response, and the reason for it, should represent the classic attitude of artist toward critic. A work of art is untranslatable. The symbols that it contains are their own best form—in Yeats's thought, their only *possible* form. It would make as much sense to ask a statesman to translate an international treaty into heroic couplets in order to understand it, as to assume that rephrasings or glosses are adequate substitutes for—let alone improvements upon— successful symbols.

Yeats does not wish to limit the suggestibility of the symbol. Like a tree, a symbol has roots in unseen depths, branches that allow air from far places to play upon it. "It is only by ancient symbols," he says, "by symbols that have numberless meanings beside the one or two the writer lays an emphasis upon, or the half-score he knows of, that any highly subjective art can escape from the barrenness and shallowness of a too conscious arrangement, into the abundance and depth of nature. The poet of essences and pure ideas must seek in the half-lights that glimmer from symbol to symbol as if to the ends of the earth, all that the epic and dramatic poet finds of mystery and shadow in the accidental circumstance of life." [20]

The symbol constantly expands our minds with the multiplicity of its implications. It evokes, often from the limited life of a simple fable, "the rich, far-wandering, many-imaged life of the half-seen world beyond." [21] * Though the poetic symbol is concrete, nevertheless Yeats knows that "art has never taken more than its symbols from anything that the eye can see or the hand measure." [22] Opposed to realistic art, therefore, "There is an art of the flood. . . . And we call this art poetical, because we must bring more to it than our daily mood if we would take our pleasure; and because it takes delight in the moment of exaltation, of excitement, of dreaming." [23] Rooted in tradition,[24] * in history, and in dreams, the symbols of great art take on an inexhaustible power far beyond the formal statements of their own words, far beyond any relationships rigidly held to the poem itself. In his theory and his practice, Yeats is no help to those critics who would set up a pure aesthetic judgment based on a poem as self-contained. "Tragic art," he writes, "passionate art, the drowner of dykes, the confounder of understanding, moves us by setting us to reverie, by alluring us almost to the intensity of trance. The persons upon the stage, let us say, greaten till they are humanity itself. We feel our minds expand convulsively or spread out slowly like some moon-brightened image-crowded sea." [25]

This profound, passionate, tragic art which Yeats's ideal symbols evoke is, of necessity, moral. What poet, as Yeats conceives him, can remain indifferent to Ideas of Good and Evil? Yet the poet is not moral in any narrow sense, and Yeats, indeed, has mocking words for the merely didactic.[26] * The supreme instrument of morality is the imagination, because it widens man's scope for judgment. No wonder that Yeats calls Shelley's *Defence of Poetry* "the profoundest essay on the foundation of poetry in English"! [27] * Because of his belief in the moral value of imaginative symbols, Yeats is able to praise an artist in terms that intertwine ethics and aesthetics. William Blake, he believes, learned from Jacob Boehme that "the imaginative arts were therefore the greatest of Divine revelations, and that the sympathy with all living things, sinful and righteous alike, which the imaginative arts awaken, is that forgiveness of sins commanded by Christ." [28] Even religion may be indistinguishable from the highest artistic thought, for Yeats holds that in Blake's mind "The historical Christ was indeed no more than the supreme symbol of the artistic imagination." [29] Such a high value does Yeats set upon the imaginative poet that the prophets themselves belong to a lower order.[30] *

The dignity of the artist is not of his own making. He is one of the reeds the wind blows through. The past breathes upon him, from "that great memory, which is still the mother of the Muses." [31] And he breathes upon the future, offering symbols which are part of his instinct before they are part of his knowledge. Shapers of destiny, the poetic symbols spring to mind suddenly and unexpectedly; they create themselves, and in turn create the future. "Because an emotion does not exist," Yeats writes, "or does not become perceptible and active among us, till it has found its expression, . . . and because no two modulations or arrangements . . . evoke the same emotion, poets and painters and musicians . . . are continually making and unmaking mankind." [32]

These self-creating symbols are of slow growth, like a tree. They cannot be forced, or deliberately constructed. "Any one," Yeats believes, "who has any experience of any mystical state of the soul knows how there float up in the mind profound symbols, whose meaning, if indeed they do not delude one into the dream that they are meaningless, one does not perhaps understand for years." [33] * Part of the wander-years of an artist are spent in trying to find the straight path, in discarding symbols that are not his own, in choosing those poetic ideas that belong to his life, and allowing them to mature. [34] * Often these symbols appear originally in ineffective or distorted shapes. [35] * But once truly found, they are a part of a poet's life and power. "I know," Yeats writes, "how hard it is to forget a symbolical meaning, once one has found it." [36]

These organic, slowly-growing symbols may become, as it were, the hard core of an artist's existence. They may give his life its most profound significance, its central lamp, even though they be but partially understood. "I do not think men change much in their deepest thought," [37] Yeats writes. And again: "There is for every man some one scene, some one adventure, some one picture that is the image of his secret life, for wisdom first speaks in images, and . . . this one image, if he would but brood over it his life long, would lead his soul." [38] * The central image may dominate and organize subsidiary images, giving pattern to a poet's entire work. [39] * Increasing organization so dominates Yeats's thought that he sees symbols not only as holding together one man's poems, but as uniting different poets. "A group of writers have often a per-

sistent image," [40] such as the "stars" for the poets of the
'nineties, the "bones" for modern poets.

And finally, these poetic symbols—so unified, meaningful,
complex, untranslatable, inexhaustible in suggestion, moral in
sympathy, self-creating, slow-growing, profoundly central—
must constitute little less than revelation. Obviously by now,
symbolism in Yeats's use implies a qualitative judgment, a conception of intensity and significance. All poems employ metaphors, which are accepted or fanciful symbols. Words themselves are symbols. But the metaphorical manner of poetry,
when it is most successful, needs a stronger word than mere
metaphor. "We may call this metaphorical writing," Yeats remarks, "but it is better to call it symbolical writing, because
metaphors are not profound enough to be moving, when they
are not symbols." [41] Whenever art uses these powerful and
profound symbols, then, poetry opens one of the few portals
left into Paradise. For a moment the veil of appearances
trembles, and we breathe airs from far and timeless countries.

"Everything that can be seen, touched, measured, explained,
understood, argued over, is to the imaginative artist nothing
more than a means, for he belongs to the invisible life, and
delivers its ever new and ever ancient revelation. We hear
much of his need for the restraints of reason, but the only
restraint he can obey is the mysterious instinct that has made
him an artist, and that teaches him to discover immortal moods
in mortal desires, an undecaying hope in our trivial ambitions,
a divine love in sexual passion." [42] *

Believing in the revelatory power of symbols, whereof the
poets are the priests and altar-ministrants, Yeats cannot but
treat the calling of the poet reverently, as if it were in truth
a calling and an inspiration. He says: "When a man writes any
work of genius, or invents some creative action, is it not because some knowledge or power has come into his mind from
beyond his mind? It is called up by an image, as I think; . . .

but our images must be given to us, we cannot choose them deliberately." [43]

Yeats's theory of poetry centers upon the symbol. Its complex nature he describes with consistency and coherence. His conceptions of poetry, repeatedly expressed and hinted at, have been worth developing at such length, because too many people hold either that poetry cannot be discussed, or that poetry can be completely explained in rational terms. To neither of these camps does Yeats belong. The mosaic of this essay to this point shows Yeats willing to meditate upon his art. Yet not to analyze poetry in rational abstractions. The abstract is anathema to Yeats: it kills the very life which poetry strives to intensify.

Yeats's theory of poetry is of particular interest because it was held by a man who produced the greatest poems of our lifetime. It was no easy theory to hold, to explain, or to throw into successful practice. Three great obstacles rise: the poetic symbols appear unexpectedly, without an act of the will, and grow slowly; the poetic symbols have an import and a tremendous suggestivity beyond the poet's mind; the perfect symbol is unanalyzable, so that its success must be judged almost proportionately with the failure of any explanations to satisfy: the original symbol is the thing itself, a mystical unity —meaning and image inseparable.

In short, the poetic symbols cannot be controlled; they cannot be limited; they cannot be explained.

How, then, may a practising poet proceed? Perhaps only in hope and prayer. All that he can do is to say:

> Be thou, spirit fierce,
> My spirit! Be thou me, impetuous one!

Yeats moved consciously along many paths. Many of them proved blind trails. His unconscious development, which I believe he himself would have considered more important, is worth some speculation. The straight path of the intellect and the will is, in his philosophy, not the shortest way home. The road of the chameleon, *Hodos Chameleontos*, is one of his persistent thoughts. This is the winding road of instinctive life, changing colors and directions, the path through a world in which the values are not fixed and certain and universal.

To see his poetic theory in practice, one procedure might be to trace the slow development of a symbol. Almost any of his symbols will do, for the important ones persist and grow in clarity, and their intertwining makes any one of them but a part of the whole tree—the leaf, the blossom, or the bole. Arbitrarily, let us take Yeats's symbol of the gyre or spiral, and assume that it is connected with man's intellect. Let us begin with speculation on some of his persisting instincts and beliefs; then turn to some early forms of the symbol expressing these convictions; and finally follow through their development and changes to a late use in a complete poem.

Many of Yeats's thoughts cluster around tradition, ceremony, custom, the great memory of the past. Moments of intense passion and significance live on, or recur. The transmigration of a soul through many lives is possible. Human history is a great, ever-returning pattern, a formal dance. No traditionalist, no man so skeptical of the power of unaided reason as was Yeats, will easily be swept away by ideas of progress. Instead of the straight line of progress, Yeats's instincts would naturally turn to the closed circle. To the cyclical theory of history his convictions would easily respond. Moreover, attracted by the permanent and not the transient, he might easily see, with Plato, the sphere or circle as the emblem of eternity, since a circle is without beginning or ending. A spiral might fit his thought even more closely when he thinks of history, since in the spiral a return to the same general position is possible,

but on a slightly different plane—as if, say, the horizontal
dimensions represented the permanent, the vertical dimension
the transient, in a three-dimensional temporal system that included both.

In his own personal thought, Yeats needed a symbol for introspection, for the mind turning in upon itself. Here again,
the image of the spinning gyres, the humming sleeping top,
might prove effective. And as a respecter of the past, binding
his own days each to each by natural piety, if he could only
find some image from his own childhood experience, would
his needed symbol not acquire thereby a greater authenticity
and solidity?

He found what he needed in the word "pern." How many
people who had not read Yeats would understand the
couplet:

> He unpacks the loaded pern
> Of all 'twas pain or joy to learn?
> —"Shepherd and Goatherd," 1919.

The average dictionary is silent on "pern". Yeats helps us with
a note on this poem: "When I was a child at Sligo I could see
above my grandfather's trees a little column of smoke from
'the pern mill,' and was told that 'pern' was another name for
the spool, as I was accustomed to call it, on which thread was
wound. One could not see the chimney for the trees, and the
smoke looked as if it came from the mountain, and one day a
foreign sea-captain asked me if that was a burning mountain."

"Pern," then, satisfies the artist's desire for a personal symbol.
It becomes easy enough, once we know what it means; and
Yeats learns not to permit himself ordinarily the luxury of
idiosyncratic symbols whose meaning can be known only to
their inventor. He says in a note to his volume *The Winding
Stair* (1933) that he compares winding stairs in symbolic towers
to the philosophical gyres, and adds: "but it is hardly neces-

sary to interpret what comes from the main track of thought
and expression." The gyre for him, then, is on the main track of
thought and expression.[44] *

When we think of someone traveling in a spiral, or climbing
a winding staircase, proceeding from one side to the opposite
and back again, we find that the circle or the spiral is a fit
vehicle for Yeats's notions of antitheses and antinomies, as
when we speak of two objects being "diametrically opposed."
It gives him also a vehicle that he can manipulate variously to
express the tensions of desire, that dominant quality in Yeats's
conception of human life. Always for Yeats, the object of desire, the Mask, is straight across the circle from the desirer, the
Will.

Not only many of these ideas, but two symbols as well, interlock in a pair of lines:

> Though I had long perned in the gyre,
> Between my hatred and desire . . .
> —"Demon and Beast," 1921.

Association of symbols becomes so habitual that he will marry
them even when their symbolic use is not important:

> . . . To watch a white gull take
> A bit of bread thrown up into the air;
> Now gyring down and perning there . . .
> —"Demon and Beast," 1921.

The gyre leads off one of his most powerful poems, "The
Second Coming" (1921):

> Turning and turning in the widening gyre
> The falcon cannot hear the falconer;
> Things fall apart; the centre cannot hold.

And the wedded symbols are crucial in the best known of his
great poems, "Sailing to Byzantium" (1928). Here, after he

has used water imagery for youth and life, he turns to fire, stone, and metal imagery for age and intellect and art, seeing himself standing in the great church of Sancta Sophia in Constantinople, with its mosaic saints on the walls:

O sages standing in God's holy fire
As in the gold mosaic of a wall,
Come from the holy fire, perne in a gyre,
And be the singing-masters of my soul.

It is difficult to keep to the main track of thought, for "The Second Coming" draws us toward the associated symbol of the falcon, and "Sailing to Byzantium" leads us aside to wondering on what this gold, this stone, this fire may represent. But we have enough to do not to grow dizzy with the gyres. The uses of "pern" and "gyre" have been drawn from his mature work. Indeed, one of the most striking phenomena of Yeats's development is the growing clarity of his symbols as their intensity of meaning crystallizes.[45] *

Fully to understand the meaning of "gyre" in one of his later poems, all of its uses in earlier poems must ideally be in our minds—not only when the word itself is used, but when its various synonyms occur, and perhaps most important, when it is only half-suggested, or left as a hidden image, not fully developed, but controlling the movement of the thought. We would then be able to watch "gyre" expand into circles and winding stairs and cones and spirals, or into verbs such as whirl or wind or unwind. We would see "pern" open, like a multifoliate rose, into spindle, bobbin, spool, skein, spinning-jenny and spinning-top.[46] *

Although the primary use of "gyre" is perhaps to suggest the cyclical theory of history—that ages recur—such a reading would quickly show that this one symbol, or this group of symbols, cannot be understood alone. The gyre is always getting tangled, bound and wound, with other symbols. When the gyre suggests thought and introspection, it is sure to have near it some stony or deathlike image to bring out the permanent quality in works of intellect or art, for as Yeats writes: "I had noticed *once again* how all thought among us is frozen into 'something other than human life.' " [47] And often, to intensify the idea of the gyre as philosophical thought or impersonal cosmic history, Yeats will couple it with a contrasting image of cloth or of "only a woman's hair," as a symbol of sensuous individual life. Though even here, the woman's hair cannot remain a simple symbol, but takes on its own antithesis as it becomes a permanent constellation in the skies—"Berenice's burning hair." Thus the image of the gyre becomes a hidden symbol in lines such as

> But know your hair was bound and wound
> About the stars and moon and sun.
> > —"He Wishes His Beloved Were
> > Dead," 1899.[48] *

By means of this complexity-through-association, Yeats can combine the *ideas* of death, of intellect, of permanence, of individual vitality, and of recurrence or reincarnation, with the *symbols* of stony stillness, of cloth, of the pern and of the gyre, in two lines:

> Wound in mind's pondering
> As mummies in the mummy-cloth are wound.
> > —"All Souls' Night," 1928.[49] *

This is not accident. One might quote just as easily the ganglion of images in two lines from "Byzantium" (1933):

> For Hades' bobbin bound in mummy-cloth
> May unwind the winding path.

Is not some such analysis—or at any rate, the unconscious assimilation of his symbols through many readings—necessary to understand the power of a short six-line poem such as the following?

> Things out of perfection sail,
> And all their swelling canvas wear,
> Nor shall the self-begotten fail
> Though fantastic men suppose
> Building-yard and stormy shore,
> Winding-sheet and swaddling-clothes.
>
> —"Old Tom Again," No. XXIV
> of *Words for Music Perhaps*,
> 1933.

Here it is as necessary to know what Yeats has done with the *images* of the sea, of cloth, and of mummy-cloth, as to recognize the *idea* of the soul as self-begetting, to know that Plotinus had written, and Yeats had read, that "soul is the author of all living things." A "winding-sheet" in Yeats's poem is something more than three convenient syllables. The hyphen in that word marries in his mind two extensive and complex regions of speculation.

So far we have followed the symbol of the gyre in whatever involutions came up through association, hoping that we might unwind the winding path. Now let us summarize Yeats's practice in three principles:

1. All his symbols are complex.
2. Associated symbols increase the complexity of any one of his symbols.
3. Antithetical symbols increase the intensity and significance of any one of his symbols.

Here are a few illustrations of these principles. As he grew older, Yeats came to use well-known characters as symbols. The more familiar they were, the more accessible their significance to many readers. Yet since they were characters or persons, they might stand for more than one quality. Thus

Solomon might stand for wisdom; he might also stand, if one thought of the Queen of Sheba, for love or desire. Thus, Empedocles might stand for philosophy in general. He might stand for the principle of desire or the principle of opposites, since he held that the whole world was governed by love and by hate, attraction and repulsion. He might stand for alternating periods of order and chaos, as one or the other of these two principles of love and hate ruled. Or he might stand for the idea of transmigration, the recurrence of souls, which he as well as Pythagoras held. He might stand for all of these ideas and more, though the context will usually show which idea or ideas Yeats's mind considers as dominant. By using traditional figures, Yeats is able to achieve at a stroke clarity and complexity within the compression demanded by his lyrical forms.

Complexity is increased by associated images. Empedocles, for instance, becomes a more effective symbol of thought and philosophy when we are aware of Yeats's use of Pythagoras and Plato and Plotinus and the Babylonian mathematicians. The world changing at the birth of Leda's children increases in suggestive power when we know how Yeats parallels this with the world changing at the birth of Christ. Gyres, representing thought in its introspection, may be associated with stone, representing the permanent nature of thought. And this immobile stony quality of fossilized thought may be given complexity-through-variation if, in a single poem, the stone symbol might be expressed as "Old Rocky Face" (What do we have here? The Sphinxlike beast of "The Second Coming"? Or memories of native Irish mountains, Ben Bulben perhaps, which Yeats associated with supernatural happenings?), "painted forms," "ancient tombs," "cavern," "marble," "sepulchre."

A system of thought may be superposed on ordinary unsystematic thought in order to make association between symbols clearer. In terms commonly understood, Yeats may make a parallel between the violent rebirth of the world in the time of Troy and the time of Christ, in order to present a cyclical theory of history. Or he may make the same point in terms of his own system by referring to new life rising from exhausted life at the dark of the moon. Again, if Yeats were to praise "The workman, noble and saint," one might think in common reference of the medieval Three Estates, or of Chaucer's plowman, knight, and parson; or just as legitimately, one might think of Yeats's personal reverence for tradition and ceremony, or of his belief that old and gracious times in the great cycles will come back again.

And finally, conflicting symbols set off the powers of each. Opposed to the ganglions that suggest intellect, art, and age, symbolized by the gyre and the stone, are ganglions that suggest passion, life, and youth, symbolized by the sea and animal blood.[50] * The old quiescence of stone and tomb stands out more clearly if opposed violently to "blood and mire" and "numb nightmare" and "sensitive body"; "thought" may be set more clearly against "beauty" and passionate life, if beauty is further enriched, thought opposed, by images of "Lovers of horses and of women," by "the polecat and the owl."

These illustrations of the three principles underlying Yeats's use of symbols should help to understand his late poem called "The Gyres" (*Last Poems and Plays*, 1940):

> The gyres! the gyres! Old Rocky Face, look forth;
> Things thought too long can be no longer thought,
> For beauty dies of beauty, worth of worth,
> And ancient lineaments are blotted out.
> Irrational streams of blood are staining earth;
> Empedocles has thrown all things about;
> Hector is dead and there's a light in Troy;
> We that look on but laugh in tragic joy.

What matter though numb nightmare ride on top,
And blood and mire the sensitive body stain?
What matter? Heave no sigh, let no tear drop,
A greater, a more gracious time has gone;
For painted forms or boxes of make-up
In ancient tombs I sighed, but not again;
What matter? Out of cavern comes a voice,
And all it knows is that one word 'Rejoice!'

Conduct and work grow coarse, and coarse the soul,
What matter? Those that Rocky Face holds dear,
Lovers of horses and of women, shall,
From marble of a broken sepulchre,
Or dark betwixt the polecat and the owl,
Or any rich, dark nothing disinter
The workman, noble and saint, and all things run
On that unfashionable gyre again.

The idea in the poem is simple. It may be paraphrased in two
lines from Dryden's *Secular Masque* (I had almost written
Cyclical Masque):

> 'Tis well an old age is out
> And time to begin a new.

Yet it is given its richness and suggestiveness through the interlocking and opposing symbols. The line near the end of the
first stanza:

> Hector is dead and there's a light in Troy

is reinforced by the coming of a new age at the end of the
second:

> Out of cavern comes a voice
> And all it knows is that one word 'Rejoice!'

And this reference to the risen Christ and the empty tomb is made clearer in the third:

> From marble of a broken sepulchre.[51] *

Yeats describes a single situation in three superposed (or spiraled) planes of time: the age of Troy, the age of Christ, and the present age. The idea of a new age is formally reinforced by giving in it two further alternative images drawn from Yeats's own conception of a new cycle coming in with the dark of the moon—the absolute, abstract phase in his system, which is followed by the first crescent and the beginnings of new human life:

> Or dark betwixt the polecat and the owl
> Or any rich, dark nothing.

It is too much to expect that the creations on which a gifted artist concentrates his life may be understood by his less gifted readers and critics in an hour. Perhaps this dwelling upon the one symbol of the gyres has merely made it more bewildering. Only through a stage of initial bewilderment, however, only through increasing realization of complexity, may one arrive at a reading of Yeats which seems both clear and comprehensive. I should say, of course, *more* clear and comprehensive, for certainly this talk of the gyres must seem too long drawn out and at the same time too sketchy. To set one of Yeats's symbols in its place is simply to point our relations with other symbols and other thoughts; and to trace all of their implications, it is hardly too much to say, would require a close scrutiny of his entire work. Here is Yeats's mastery—the extraordinary coherence and persistence of his thought, which fosters the extraordinary suggestiveness of each symbol.

His own theory of poetry was wrought with deliberate intensity. The poetic process for him centered on the use of the symbol, upon which he placed impossible burdens: that it should contain a meaning and yet a meaning inseparable from its expression; that it should suggest within itself its own opposite; that its precision should not mar its inexhaustible power of suggestion; that it should bear a relation to an artist's entire career, yet that it should draw its force from the great springs of life over which an artist has no control. Here are luck and cunning mixed. Here is the poet at once the conscious artist and the trumpet of a revelation.

Yet out of blood and stone, Yeats constructs art. He murders impossibilities, and makes his enamelled nightingale sing as if it were a living bird. "Miracle, bird, or golden handiwork!" [52] we may well wonder. And we may decide: "More miracle than bird or handiwork." In his hands, artificial and theoretical symbols actually work and sing with life. If all poets were as clear and vigorous and consistent in their thought, if all theorists on poetry were as lucky and gifted and original in their practice, then the phenomenon of a great poet living in our time would not seem so close to miracle.

CHAPTER THREE

THE READING OF A LYRIC

"What I tell you three times is true."
—*Old Song.*

"He who finds out a new pleasure is one of the most
useful members of society."
—GOLDSMITH, *Letters from a Citizen
of the World*, Number XI.

STYLES in the arts change. We have all of us long been aware
of that fact—perhaps too much aware, so that the literary historians produce the fantastic illusion that literature is created,
not by the poet, but by our modern equivalent for the Nine
Muses, allegorical somethings called Influence, Indebtedness,
Trend, Period, Source, Convention, Genre, Parallel Passage,
and Style.

Yeats felt that style was an unmistakable individual voice.
But "style" is a slippery word. Frequently it is used (this may
be seen most clearly in the criticism of the visual arts) to indicate the manner of creation of an entire period. Just as we
speak of styles in dress, we may speak of the baroque style,
or the neo-classic style, or the abstract style of modern art.
And we are conscious that whole ages may fall generally into
such manners or mannerisms in artistic creation. In the criticism of painting, "Mannerism" even denotes a particular historical style!

What we do not accept as obvious is that the reception of art is equally mannered. If a work is solely alive, or most alive, as Samuel Butler somewhere says, on "the lips of living men," then we should pay some attention to its auditors, its executants, its recipients. The words of a poem on a page are merely the score for a piece of music; the music itself quickens in the minds of its readers. It might be possible, for example, to draw up at least a shadowy history of how English poetry has been read and received. It might be possible to indicate answers to such questions as these: Did the Renaissance judge a poem somewhat mechanically by classifying it in its form, by assigning it a grade for its didactic success, and by counting the number of tropes and rhetorical figures its cunning author employed? Why did eighteenth-century readers tend to reduce every poem to abstract virtues, and laud it as nervous, correct, manly, perspicuous, natural? How could the nineteenth century appraise the response to poetry with any clarity at all, under the influence of romantic "enthusiasm" and the doctrine of the imagination, which tended to veto detailed analysis as the whittling of little minds?

And what of the twentieth century? This era of ours has developed psychology and sociology, for all the good and bad they can do. The sociological approach may here be omitted, for in one sense Yeats's entire career was devoted to opposing a conception so deadening to literary values. But the psychological approach is of tremendous importance, particularly with regard to this new awareness of how a poem affects, not its creator, but the reader who gives it all its career after birth. The three wise men at the cradle of modern criticism are Benedetto Croce, I. A. Richards, and T. S. Eliot. Croce made literary criticism a branch of philosophy, developing Kant's theories until it was clear that the work of art was a unique and therefore an incomparable experience. Richards approached art as a psychologist, and found by practical experiments what art did to those who perceived it, or at least tried to perceive it. And Eliot, though he contributed little new in theory, walked the road of the chameleon in criticism as Yeats did in poetry, and kept criticism alive by tentative judgments and by sensitive responses to the highest art in any form.

Among the followers of this triumvirate, modern poetic criticism has become perhaps too codified, too rigid, too exclusive. The practice of Eliot and Joyce has often made the art of criticism into a recondite guessing game, in which bright young men who contemn the older types of scholarship carry those same types to a further extreme in tracing down everything which their author may have read or been influenced by. Misunderstanding Croce's sharp philosophical distinction that makes aesthetic an autonomous study, the poets have gone on to assume that logic and ethic are not in *any* sense parts of the aesthetic intuition; the result has been *la poésie pure*—as if the aesthetic experience could take place in a void! They have disregarded Croce's own impressive respect for the value of history, both particular and general history, and have written poems non-historical, non-logical, non-moral, which in their deliberate separation from life must eventually result in life being separated from them.

In literary criticism, the best of our recent critics have followed one of two paths, and sometimes have walked along them both. One method depends upon the assumption that a work of art is self-contained. Croce's philosophical theory gives some base for such an assumption; and Richards, obviously disgusted with the academic habit of telling a reader what he should think of a poem and know about it and its age and its author before it is even read, put the idea into practice by giving his students unnamed and unknown poems to analyze. The other method depends upon setting up standards of what a poem ought to be. This must always be (though it never seems so to the critics who practice it) a matter of personal rather than universal taste. Richards points out our complex appetencies, and makes some most acute observations about the place of irony in a great tragic work of art; Eliot helps in the refurbishing of Donne, admires the Elizabethan dramatists, and introduces to the English-speaking world the astringent clashing of certain French poets. What is the result? Irony, drama, tension, shock-technique, become the sole standards by which to judge the worth of a poem.

Yet what poet should be judged in the shadow—I will not say the light—of any other poet? Is Robert Bridges' Olympian languor beneath notice because he is blind to the coiled springs in Hopkins? On what grounds is one form of blindness preferable to another? Is frenzy, because it is disastrous for Tennyson, to be censured in William Blake? On what safer basis do we rule out Shelley as deficient in irony than the Victorians ruled out Donne as lacking in mellifluousness? Is not the late Shakespeare so different a man from the early Shakespeare that neither *Love's Labour's Lost* nor *The Tempest* should be judged with the other play as a standard? If the poet's is a personal voice, criticism is not making for a full choir by insisting that all poets should sing on the same note, even if that note were demonstrably the base of the scale and there were only one possible scale.

This chapter does not contemplate setting up an exclusive theory of poetry. It merely will attempt to deny other exclusive theories on the grounds that they do not explain one particular poet, William Butler Yeats. And it will of course not deny them *in toto*, but merely *in partibus*, for this is an age of vigorous pioneering criticism, in which all trails across the frontier should be followed right up to the fork where they seem to be leading away from the high mountains, or the as yet unsurveyed ranges. The negative aspects of this chapter

are two, and are incidental: the theory of the self-sufficiency
of a work of art does not do justice to Yeats's poems; the
theory that all art is dramatic and ironic is disastrously inadequate to explain the greatness of Yeats's lyrics.

Positively, the argument should demonstrate how necessary
to the understanding of any one poem of Yeats is some knowledge of at least the main body of his poems. (His life and his
literary sources are outside the scope of this book.) And it
should show that through his technique of echoing and repetition and allusion to his own work, through his conception of
marmorean stillness, Yeats has built his characteristic pieces—
consciously, and for the first time in English literature with
complete success—to a point where the lyric, that slight form
if words alone are counted, is on an equal plane with the epic
and the drama in dignity and power.

What poet in the range of literature in English has done as
much as Yeats to elevate the status of the lyric?

Yeats was aware at an early stage that a poem is not an
isolated event; it is a momentary reading in time, but it inevitably implies, in the artist's thought at least, what has gone
before and may come after. It is his signature for a particular
occasion, but it is as personal as a signature, and will resemble
his other signatures. Yeats's theory, developed sometimes consciously, sometimes instinctively, sometimes through the practice of poetry, may be clearly seen in his essay on "The Philosophy of Shelley's Poetry," [1] written when Yeats was thirty-
five. He reads and broods over Shelley's poems until he finds
the meanings of their symbols, meanings which in single poems
might not reveal their complexity or clarity. "Water," Yeats
writes, "is his great symbol of existence." "Alastor calls the
river that he follows an image of his mind." "The tower . . .
is, like the sea, and rivers, and caves with fountains, a very ancient symbol." Here the symbols are beginning their interplay; they are seen in relation to each other. "Once at any

rate," Yeats writes of Shelley's poetic method, "a tower is used to symbolize a meaning that is contrary to the meaning symbolized by caves."

Furthermore, each symbol may have ambiguous or multiplex meanings. Shelley's cave or cavern, as Yeats sees it, is sometimes man's mind, sometimes his youth, sometimes the mysteries after death, or an enclosed life, or "the still cave of poetry." He adds significantly: "and it may have all meanings at once." A poet gradually comes to adopt as his own the symbols from which his instincts cannot escape. The Moon, which "is the most changeable of symbols, and not merely because it is the symbol of change . . . is not loved by the children of desire." Keats appropriates the Moon, as Blake in his energy takes over the Sun. But Shelley is a child of desire, and therefore Yeats imagines that he "would have wandered, lost in a ceaseless reverie, in some chapel of the Star of infinite desire."

Only very slowly does a poet discover his own symbols. "Any one who has any experience of any mystical state of the soul knows how there float up in the mind profound symbols, whose meaning, if indeed they do not delude one into the dream that they are meaningless, one does not perhaps understand for years." But an artist's personality is unwavering— "I do not think men change much in their deepest thought"— and once discovered, the artist may build from his symbols a house without hands, in which he may rest at home. "I know how hard it is to forget a symbolical meaning, once one has found it." "There is for every man some one scene, some one adventure, some one picture that is the image of his secret life, for wisdom first speaks in images, and . . . this one image, if he would but brood over it his life long, would lead his soul." For Shelley, the Morning and Evening Star "is the throne of his genius."

The reader will probably already have remarked that some of Shelley's symbols Yeats made his own—the tower, the sea, the fountain—while others (the star and the river, for example) never became his hallmarks. Yeats is aware of possible comparisons between Shelley's images and his own: "the wolf is but a more violent symbol of longing and desire than the hound," so that Shelley's wolf reminds Yeats of the hound and the deer that Usheen saw, the hound which Yeats uses so frequently in his stories and poems and which, uncharacteristically, he defines precisely in a note as a plain image "of the desire of the man 'which is for the woman.' " [2] Obviously, Yeats is carrying his theory further: a symbol is not the sole property of a single poem, but the communal property of all of a poet's work. More than that, it does not belong to the poet himself, but to the Great Mind of his race or culture—it belongs to tradition, if the reader shies at Yeats's particular terms of the Great Mind and the Great Memory. Therefore, to illuminate Shelley's use of caves and fountains, Yeats speaks of Homer's cave in Ithaca, or of Porphyry's Cave of the Nymphs, and adds: "He contends that fountains and rivers symbolize generation." It does not matter whether the "he" refers to Homer or Porphyry or Shelley (or for that matter, to Mr. Taylor or Mr. Lang, translators); the thought belongs to them all, but is none of their own. The climax of Yeats's faith in the communal or traditional symbol comes in the passage:

"It is only by ancient symbols, by symbols that have numberless meanings beside the one or two the writer lays an emphasis upon, or the half-score he knows of, that any highly subjective art [the lyric?] can escape from the barrenness and shallowness of a too conscious arrangement, into the abundance and depth of nature. The poet of essences and pure ideas [the lyric poet?] must seek in the half-lights that glimmer from symbol to symbol as if to the ends of the earth, all that the epic and dramatic poet finds of mystery and shadow in the accidental circumstance of life."

In this essay on Shelley, written before he had come into his own creative maturity, Yeats adumbrates his practice:

1. Every poet demands and creates his own personal language of "ruling symbols."

2. Such symbols increase their effectiveness through relation to other symbols.

3. These personal symbols may be better understood in any one poem in proportion to our knowledge of the poet's use of the same symbols elsewhere—just as a new word, though it may establish its meaning in a sentence through context, is more certainly and fully grasped after it has become an old familiar word in many contexts.

4. Symbols gain further in power and complexity when they go beyond the individual poet and take on other meanings from other minds.

Why does Yeats place such emphasis upon symbolism? Why does he hold allegory to be a lower form? Popularly considered, an allegory depends upon a story, a symbol upon a visual pattern. Yeats's instinct turns naturally to space, and when he broods upon time, he must throw his meditations into spatial metaphors. It is not without interest that his father and brother were painters, and that he grew up in a household and small society where the talk must have been more often about the visual arts than about literature. His technique for the evocation of trances is also perhaps important: he drew mystical signs, gazed at them until he was taken out of this world, went to sleep with a sprig of hawthorn on his pillow, conjured up water by thinking of a triangle. He writes:

"I dream of clear water, perhaps two or three times (the moon of the poem ["To D. W."]), then come erotic dreams. Then for weeks perhaps I will write poetry with sex for theme. Then comes the reversal—it came when I was young with some dream or some vision between waking and sleep with a flame in it. Then for weeks I got a symbolism like that in my Byzantium poem, or in 'To D. W.' with flame for theme. All this may come from the chance that when I was a young man I was accustomed to a Kabalistic ceremony where there were two pillars, one symbolic of water and one of fire. The first mark is Δ, the water mark is Δ, these are combined to make Solomon's seal ✡. The water is sensation, peace, night, silence, indolence; the fire is passion, tension, day, music, energy." [3]

This passage is quoted at length because it makes so melodramatically clear how Yeats's mature mind reduced the most complex and tenuous emotions, sensations, and ideas to spatial patterns—in this case to a couple of the simplest geometric figures antithetically related and superposed. His theories of personality and of historical time take shape as the great patterns of the wheel and of the phases of the Moon in *A Vision*. To a mind unresponsive to signs—whether those signs are geometrical figures, or the flight of birds, or the zodiacal signs of astrology—the Yeats of *A Vision* must seem, almost, at times, like some Madame Sosostris with a wicked pack of cards. Yet always the drift of his mind was toward organization, and still more organization coupled with greater simplicity. He is an Einstein in poetry, seeking for the single formula that will embrace and relate all imaginative phenomena. The single poem, even when written by one of his favorite masters, is not enough; it is but a fragment. No wonder, then, that he can say of Shelley: "I only made my pleasure in him contented pleasure by massing in my imagination his recurring images of towers and rivers, and caves with fountains in them, and that one star of his, till his world had grown solid underfoot and consistent enough for the soul's habitation." [4]

The dean of poets writing in English, the older Yeats devoted much time and energy to selecting the poems published in 1936 as *The Oxford Book of Modern Verse 1892–1935*. As an even-handed representation of recent English poetry it is a disaster. A dramatist can anthologize fairly (what else is dialogue among persons than an anthology?), but a lyric poet has trouble. Yeats's strong and certain taste builds a book of verse beautifully coherent and completely unrepresentative, from its beginning with Pater set as free verse, to the overemphasis on his friends near the end. But when modern verse becomes passive, or realistic, or fearful, or low-keyed, or disjointed, or jagged, Yeats the lyric master of passionate convictions simply disregards it. "Form," he says in his Olympian *Introduction*, "must be full, sphere-like, single."

At the beginning and end of his career, then, his natural instincts were toward pattern, toward revelation through visual evocation. He is a descendant of the Pre-Raphaelite poet-painters, who wrote pictures and painted sonnets. Art for Yeats is a vision; at times it is almost geometry. To such a mind, the story is nothing, the image is everything, "the image of his secret life."

But, it may be objected, in the middle of the road of his life, Yeats gave almost a score of years to the theatre. How could such a theorist write drama? The answer is, of course, that Yeats rarely did. At least in any sense that would be popularly recognized. He wrote lyric poems in dialogue, built dreams in which named figures speak; and sometimes these enchantments were put on the stage. If quantitative measurement of genius were possible, no doubt it could be shown that Yeats spent more time and energy worrying over his narrative and dramatic poems and constructing his *Vision* than on all his lyric poems put together. But the gifts of genius are unpredictable, and the judgment of history may well be that the world should be grateful to Yeats for such long work over the dramas and the philosophical system simply as scaffoldings and sketches that made his lyrical achievement so bright and clear.

His dramatic criticism and theory show that his bent was not truly dramatic. Even when he talks about plays, he is continually reducing them to the condition of music. In his essays on "Certain Noble Plays of Japan" (1916) and "The Tragic Theatre" (1910), he is constantly making tragedy a synonym for poetry, and limiting poetry to the lyric mode. Repetition and pattern, the formal movement of a minuet, the analogies with painting and with lyric poetry, recur in his thought. It is hardly too much to say that he finds models in Oriental drama, toward which his own practice unconsciously tended, precisely for those qualities which Occidentals would consider *not* dramatic. He thinks that he discovers in the Japanese Noh plays "a playing upon a single metaphor, as deliberate as the echoing rhythm of line in Chinese and Japanese painting." [5] And to follow, he chooses as a parallel the most unlikely and undramatic of English poets: "In European poetry I remember Shelley's continually repeated fountain and cave, his broad stream and solitary star." Immobile ecstasy is his demand. This hardly makes for good drama. In Shakespeare's tragedies and tragicomedies, "amid the great moments . . . all is lyricism, unmixed passion, 'the integrity of fire.' " [6]

Except as a set for chanting, pageantry, and ceremonious dances, of what use is the stage to Yeats? He praises actors for their exquisite reading of lines, their hieratic gestures, their "beautiful fantasy"; one of his dedications is to Edmund Dulac because that painter did a fine set and masks for one of Yeats's little plays. A ballet master or an orchestra conductor could more easily understand Yeats's effects than a practical producer. In Yeats's last play, *The Death of Cuchulain*,[7] the Old Man who produces it says of its three musicians: "I will teach them, if I live, the music of the beggar-man, Homer's music. I promise a dance. I wanted a dance because where there are no words there is less to spoil." All art is still tending toward the condition of music. In *The Cat and the*

Moon (1926) the three musicians actually outnumber the actors.

Deliberately Yeats keeps "persons" out of his plays. You would not recognize one of his characters on the street or as next-door neighbor. But *objects* almost become fetishes: the crucifix in *The Land of Heart's Desire*, the treasure in *The Countess Cathleen*, the magic stone in *The Pot of Broth*, food in *The King's Threshold*, the coach in *The Unicorn from the Stars*. Symbols often overshadow the poor actors—the heron and the moon in *Calvary*, the unicorn in *The Player-Queen*, the great painted figure of the hawk in *At the Hawk's Well*, the cat and the moon in the play justly titled *The Cat and the Moon*. How much flesh-and-blood actuality would one expect in a play precisely called *The Dreaming of the Bones*?

Many of the plays have their vital action beyond the stage. The unicorn comes *from* the stars and motivates the play through a trance. The principal figures in the fascinating *Words Upon the Window Pane* are Jonathan Swift and Stella and Vanessa; since it is laid in modern times, they never appear on the stage, but speak through the voice of a medium at a séance. The leading forces in *The Only Jealousy of Emir* and *The Countess Cathleen* are otherworldly and do not come upon the stage. In *At the Hawk's Well* nothing happens. *The Dreaming of the Bones* is set at the time of the 1916 Irish rebellion, yet its passion is the remembrance of the unhappy traitorous ghosts Dermot and Dervorgilla who brought the Normans into Ireland seven hundred years before. Stylization is carried so far that in *The Death of Cuchulain*, the war goddess, the Morrigu, dances with a black parallelogram which represents a man's head.

Songs, musicians, dances, the folding and unfolding of painted cloths, masks. Is such a collection recognizable as furnishing the materials for modern drama? The last three of Aristotle's six elements of tragedy, and the least important in his eyes—diction, music, and spectacle—seem to have taken over the stage. Partly this is Yeats's conscious revulsion against the trivialities of modern realism. Ibsen seems automatically to have made him sick, and he was disappointed in the later development toward realism of the Irish theatre. He can be courteously biting about Shaw; he can be devastatingly silent about many playwrights when they rouse no interest or sympathy in him. Partly it is his aristocratic sense of the possible heights of the drama which may be attained through the tragic reading of verse, tragic stylization in acting, tragic dancing. His old man producer of *The Death of Cuchulain* says: "I spit three times. I spit upon the dancers painted by Degas. I spit upon their short bodices, their stiff stays, their toes whereon they spin like peg-tops, above all upon that chambermaid face." [8] To balance the vulgarity of Degas' models, Yeats says elsewhere: "An actor of passion will display some one quality of soul, personified again and again, just as a great poetical painter, Titian, Botticelli, Rossetti, may depend for his greatness upon a type of beauty which presently we call by his name." [9]

The wheel has come full circle, and in spite of ourselves we are back at a discussion of painters in order to illustrate some point of the drama. Yeats is incorrigibly a lyric poet whose imagination is set in vivid symbolic visual patterns, and it is no good talking drama with him in other terms. Yet how is it possible to place what he was trying to do in the theatre? He detests abstractions; he also detests realism. What does he strive for?

He strives for passion, which might be described, in his conception, as the moment of such intensity that it escapes from time and from personality and becomes a part of the common human heritage. Set such passions against one another or in relationship, and a pattern is formed which may have significance. And the significant pattern, the overarching symbol, may serve as a model for aspiration, a guiding light for a nation's spirit. In his autobiographies, Yeats says that as a young man he tried to conceive a Unity of Culture defined and evoked by Unity of Image. He adds: "I asked no help of books, for I believed that the truth I sought would come to me like the subject of a poem, from some moment of passionate experience." [10] * This moment of passion must be given permanence and pattern. "The end of art," he writes, "is the ecstasy awakened by the presence before an ever-changing mind of what is permanent in the world, or by the arousing of that mind itself into the very delicate and fastidious mood habitual with it when it is seeking those permanent and recurring things." [11] The artist, therefore, sets aside his own personality and works by all discoverable means toward loftiness, toward "marmorean stillness." [12] * The masks which Yeats demands for his actors in so many of his plays are merely further signs of this desire to refine away all personal and distracting details in order to increase impersonal tragic passion. He writes, using an initial phrase which suggests again the embodying of that which is unchanging: "Only by the substantiation of the soul I thought, whether in literature or in sanctity, can we come upon those agreements, those separations from all else[,] that fasten men together lastingly." [13]

The impersonal purifications of passion are given nobility and pattern through oppositions: "I think that all noble things are the result of warfare; great nations and classes, of warfare in the visible world, great poetry and philosophy, of invisible warfare, the division of a mind within itself, a victory, the sacrifice of a man to himself." [14] The life of an individual or of a nation comes from this sacrifice of personality to an ideal— the ceaseless yearning toward a pattern which is of all things not impossible the most difficult: "And as I look backward upon my own writing, I take pleasure alone in those verses where it seems to me I have found something hard and cold, some articulation of the Image, which is the opposite of all that I am in my daily life, and all that my country is; yet man or nation can no more make this Mask or Image than the seed can be made by the soil into which it is cast." [15] In the case of an artist, this opposition is further complicated, since now not only is the ideal "Mask" opposed to his personal "Will," but the accident of existence, his "Body of Fate," is opposed to his shaping imagination, his "Creative Mind":

"As life goes on we discover that certain thoughts sustain us in defeat, or give us victory, whether over ourselves or others, and it is these thoughts, tested by passion, that we call convictions. Among subjective men (in all those, that is, who must spin a web out of their own bowels) the victory is an intellectual daily recreation of all that exterior fate snatches away, and so that fate's antithesis; while what I have called 'the Mask' is an emotional antithesis to all that comes out of their internal nature. We begin to live when we have conceived life as tragedy." [16]

These oppositions are not dramatic in the sense of representing a conflict between persons. They are the tensions between permanent states of the spirit. They are tragic because they keep perpetually alive man's conflict between what he desires to be and what his mortal limitations compel him to be. Life becomes for Yeats a great pattern of profound spiritual import; but drama is destroyed not merely because Yeats rules out other actors in order to touch the secret: he also wishes to annihilate himself as a personality in order to reach "those separations from all else, that fasten men together lastingly."

This marmorean stillness, this trancelike immobility, impossible as it is as a basis for drama, offers a pure and fresh source for lyric poetry. Perhaps the best short description of the Parnassian mode of Yeats's great poems would be the two words, "lyrical stasis." [17] * This is the cutting of an agate, the fashioning of "something hard and cold," the making of a poem "cold and passionate as the dawn," the "articulation of the Image," the search for "the thing that was before the world was made," [18] * the theme of "that stillness" in which personality is lost in love and the Zodiac is changed into a sphere,[19] the striving for certainty that "all's arranged in one clear view." [20] The object in all such recurring phrases and ideas is the distilling away of accidentals and the achievement of purity and stillness. Passion, purity, form, permanence become a single thing.

Yeats's idea is most difficult to convey. He is not seeking for the lowest common denominator, for he is no leveller or great commoner. He abhors abstractions when they disregard the whole from which they abstract. Rather, he is seeking the guiding principles that will keep realistic details and personal frettings from seeming important. "Passion could bring character enough." [21] Therefore boys and girls, sick for ideal imagined love, could understand Pythagoras and his theory of numbers, for calculation and measure can overcome the flux of things and give clarity. Passion is not our velleities, but the blood of our ancestors and our own measured moments of intensity.

> Measurement began our might:
> Forms a stark Egyptian thought,
> Forms that gentler Phidias wrought.[22]

The Greek sculptors that worked from ideal principles and ideal calculated proportions, created our art, substituted one image for "the many-headed," and "put down All Asiatic vague immensities.[23] And today the modern Irish, born into "that ancient sect" of intellect, calculation, number, measurement,

> may trace
> The lineaments of a plummet-measured face.[24] *

All of Yeats's art is devoted to the perfection of such universal images of sculptured stillness. Obviously the theory of a poem as self-contained is useless in judging his works, which depend for their authenticity upon past experience, personal and communal. Just as obviously, the modern theories that depend *primarily* upon irony, paradox, shifting moods, development, complexity, and drama are not applicable either, for he is seeking passionate art that burns with the integrity and simplicity of fire. His direction is that of Gertrude Stein in her famous sentence: "A rose is a rose is a rose is a rose." And if that sentence is paradoxical and dramatic, then how can anyone ever achieve undivided simple intensity?

Yeats's technical devices are devoted to sustaining the mood of lyrical stasis. He writes:

"The purpose of rhythm, it has always seemed to me, is to prolong the moment of contemplation, the moment when we are both asleep and awake, which is the one moment of creation, by hushing us with an alluring monotony, while it holds us waking by variety, to keep us in that state of perhaps real trance, in which the mind liberated from the pressure of the will is unfolded in symbols." [25] Both his rhythm and his rhyme are delicately calculated to walk the knife-edge. His rhythm does not pound with strident insistency; nor does it fall off into a formless desolate freedom, like a waste of Siberian tundra. In rhyme, he adopts neither the limiting principle of Housman's exact chiming, nor the equally limiting principle of Wilfred Owen's deliberate false-rhyme. He balances an awareness of both. Through the most minute shadings in his technique he creates a kind of metaphysical pattern that suggests man's estate, so that we are simultaneously aware of form and freedom, of immutable law and possible rebellion.

Since the achievement of poetry marks the worth of poetic theory, let us turn to a single lyric poem and read it in the light

of Yeats's thought. Consider "The Wild Swans of Coole"
(1919):

> The trees are in their autumn beauty,
> The woodland paths are dry,
> Under the October twilight the water
> Mirrors a still sky;
> Upon the brimming water among the stones
> Are nine-and-fifty swans.
>
> The nineteenth autumn has come upon me
> Since I first made my count;
> I saw, before I had well finished,
> All suddenly mount
> And scatter wheeling in great broken rings
> Upon their clamorous wings.
>
> I have looked upon those brilliant creatures,
> And now my heart is sore.
> All's changed since I, hearing at twilight,
> The first time on this shore,
> The bell-beat of their wings above my head,
> Trod with a lighter tread.
>
> Unwearied still, lover by lover,
> They paddle in the cold
> Companionable streams or climb the air;
> Their hearts have not grown old;
> Passion or conquest, wander where they will,
> Attend upon them still.
>
> But now they drift on the still water
> Mysterious, beautiful;
> Among what rushes will they build,
> By what lake's edge or pool
> Delight men's eyes when I awake some day
> To find they have flown away?

Like all the luckiest poems, this can be read with enjoyment on any of many levels. Often it gets into the anthologies, where readers may legitimately consider it as a pleasing poem on a pretty subject. The technical analysts and metrists may savor the contrasts between its feminine and masculine line-endings, may speculate on the uses of its two pairs of half rhymes, and above all may be delighted by the unanalyzable rhythm of its lines.

Those who believe a poem is self-sustaining and explicable only in its own words and form will also find rewards in "The Wild Swans"—in Yeats's cunning and almost invariable linking of each stanza to its predecessor by some repeated word or thought which modifies into a new development. They will note that the poem begins with the swans upon the lake, shifts to the images of the swans in the air, and returns to the swans on the lake—a perfect round. They will find structure in the antitheses between the swans and their beholder, and between the beholder now and the beholder nineteen years ago. And they will note (let us hope) that the essential pattern is not built in time [26] * but in a contrast between moods, and that since only mortal man in this poem feels such contrasts, the founding antithesis is between transient man and eternity.

Those who like comparative judgments may occupy themselves profitably in the parallels between the building of this poem and of, for instance, Keats's "Ode to a Nightingale." In structural devices for meditative poems of about this length, Keats and Yeats are as similar as their names.

And in this manner we might continue to invent little games of criticism, and new, or conventional, or fashionable approaches.

But what does the poem say? Everyone knows that paraphrases are inadequate. Yet a paraphrase of a poem by Yeats seems particularly thin to anyone who has read him for more than a couple of hours. Let us try it for this lyric.

In a particular place at a particular time a particular poet sees a particular number of swans. He first counted them nineteen years earlier, when they rose into the air almost before he had numbered them. He has looked upon the swans and he is sorrowful—the two statements are joined with an "and," so that he is not forcing the reader to make a causal connection if the reader doesn't care to. But at any rate, when he first heard them rise from the water, he was made happier. The swans, however, do not change. Like the "self-same song" of Keats's nightingale, the paddling or climbing of the swans goes on still; in all their wanderings, they are symbols of "passion or conquest"—or more boldly in Yeats's thought, passion and conquest are servants of the swans. Returning to the original picture of the swans drifting upon the lake in autumn, Yeats finds them mysterious as well as beautiful, and wonders whom they will delight at some future day.

Such a prose statement verges upon travesty. Yet within the strict limits of the poem it could not be built up, so long as ingenuity played fair, to the pitch of intensity which this poem rightly assumes among Yeats's other works. In structure, the poem points away from self-sufficiency: it begins with the most precise particularized stanza; by the time the next-to-the-last stanza is reached, the realm is general speculation; and the final stanza opens out, like a rich horn, into mystery, questioning, and the future.

Almost anything that is said within the formal strictures of the poem takes on more significance if Yeats's thought elsewhere is known more fully. The first two words are "The trees," and though it is of no great importance here, a whole essay might be written on Yeats's brilliant use of the tree as symbol. Criticism may be made by critics like me, but only Yeats can make a tree into the "great rooted blossomer" of "Among School Children" or into the "half all glittering flame and half all green abounding foliage" of the poem "Vacillation."

The second line speaks of "paths", but we shall not be carried aside to ask the possible relevance of the straight path of the intellect and the winding path of intuition. The paths are "dry," and perhaps that is of importance to see how earth, air, and water give structure to the poem; only the fourth element is neglected—unless the lyric itself has the simplicity of fire. We know that Yeats speculated on the meaning of the four elements and ordinarily used them with consistency. It is more than just natural history, it is symbolism, that in this poem Yeats associates the swans with water and with air. And it is more than photographic realism that Yeats is standing on the shore, the swans drifting on the water. An essay on "water" imagery in Yeats, and on "stone" imagery in opposition, would illuminate such a line as

> Upon the brimming water among the stones,

but will not be written here.

The admirer of Yeats is tempted to connect the flight of the swans, "wheeling in great broken rings," with his spiral imagery, or with the falcon turning and turning in the widening gyre; he is tempted by "the bell-beat of their wings" to run off into speculation as to why Yeats (who alludes so frequently to music yet who admits he has no ear) limits his usual references to specific musical instruments so strangely to bells and gongs. He may not be able to read the line "Among what rushes will they build," without thinking of Yeats's volume *The Wind Among the Reeds* (1899), besides a dozen other near-relevancies and associations that might possibly turn into explanations that make lines clearer.[27] *

Another almost unescapable approach is the filling in of biography; the question is naturally roused by the poem, and only the pure theorist will brush it aside in petulance. Where is Coole? What is Yeats doing there? How did he come there nineteen years ago? Why is his heart now sore? Yeats knew, and knew when he wrote the poem. Should not the reader?

I do not think it would do the reader any harm, but I am not writing a biography of William Butler Yeats. I shall choose for detailed attention a subject only relatively less complicated than the poet himself—his swans.

Nineteen years earlier, he had first seen the swans. Fifteen years earlier, in 1904, he had published a poem called "The Withering of the Boughs." [28] * It is a 24-line three-stanza poem, with a refrain that insists

> No boughs have withered because of the wintry wind;
> The boughs have withered because I have told them
>   my dreams.

The loose irregularly flowing pentameters carry with ease the sleepy leafy dreamy faery mood. There are swans in the poem; but what is more remarkable is the ganglion of associated words and images in that poem and in "The Wild Swans." Just as Shakespeare had his own sets of unexpected associations, from which according to Caroline Spurgeon it is even possible to deduce in part his personality and his experiences, so does Yeats make special patterns. The pressure is not great enough in many of them to lend them symbolic importance, but they contribute in repeated minute touches to the general texture and even to the structure, as the small *pointilliste* dots of paint in a Seurat finally add up to the outlines and massed planes of the whole painting. There are "paths" in both poems, and "streams," and a "lake," and drifting. Both are muted to the meditative mood: it is "twilight" in one, while in the other "The honey-pale moon lay low on the sleepy hills," and "the light grows cool." The contrasted ideas of wandering and of permanence are in both poems. The "mysterious" of "The Wild Swans" is matched by the "secret smile" in "The Withering of the Boughs." The "great broken rings" of the swan's flight in the later poem are present in the earlier, where the "swans fly round," and where the gyrating notion is played with variants in the "spindles of wool" of witches, or in the fairy folk who "wind and unwind dancing" on the island lawns.

The later poem is infinitely more certain and subtle. "The Withering of the Boughs" vacillates between the unconvincing fairyland of witches with crowns of pearl, and the sharp touches of curlew and peewit crying. The swans sing, whereas in the more mature poem it is the bell-beat of their clamorous wings that fires Yeats's thought. In the apprentice poem, the swans fly round somewhat embarrassingly "coupled with golden chains"; the same idea is better ordered in the later Yeats when we hear that

> Unwearied still, *lover by lover*,
> They paddle in the cold
> *Companionable* streams, or climb the air.

And the founding emotional contrast of "The Wild Swans" between the present, when the poet's heart is sore, and the past, when he trod with a lighter tread, is present in "The Withering of the Boughs," not only in the title but in the final stanza:

> I know of the sleepy country, where swans fly round
> Coupled with golden chains, and sing as they fly.
> A king and a queen are wandering there, and the sound
> Has made them so happy and hopeless, so deaf and so blind
> With wisdom, they wander till all the years have gone by.

Although these lines are fuzzily allegorical, they help in their rumpled way toward an understanding of the cold stillness of the more nearly perfect lyric. And the early poem, written so close to the original experience, may show that Yeats too creates his best poetry not in the heat of passion but in recollection long years after.

If slow maturing stamps this particular poet, then later poems as well may cast light upon "The Wild Swans at Coole." The most important are "The Tower," Part III, "Nineteen Hundred and Nineteen," Part III, "Leda and the Swan," "Among School Children," and "Coole and Ballylee, 1931." Since these are among his best poems, it is safe to assume that Yeats in crucial moments reverted to the swan as a center for his thought, a focal symbol.

Because its subject is the cyclical theory of history, or the unforeseen consequences of the moment of intense passion, "Leda and the Swan" may be dismissed here, although Zeus as the swan is the most powerful image Yeats ever developed for his "passion or conquest."

"The Tower," written in 1926, is Yeats's house and home, restored for himself and his wife; it is also the symbol of himself in his lonely pride and introspection. The short first section, with a kind of petulant disgust, admits old age; the second tries to find compensation in images and memories of the past; the third and final section concerns us here. It is Yeats's testament. He bequeaths to young upstanding men his faith and his pride. The passage on the swan is the longest and the culminating image to describe reckless, generous, open-handed "pride," and immediately precedes his declaration of "faith" in man as creator of the cosmos. These are the words:

> Pride, like that of the morn,
> When the headlong light is loose,
> Or that of the fabulous horn,
> Or that of the sudden shower
> When all streams are dry,
> Or that of the hour
> When the swan must fix his eye

Upon a fading gleam,
Float out upon a long
Last reach of glittering stream
And there sing his last song.

The section is of such importance that Yeats calls attention to
it in a note:

"In the passage about the Swan in Part III I have uncon-
sciously echoed one of the loveliest lyrics of our time—Mr.
Sturge Moore's 'Dying Swan.' I often recited it during an
American lecturing tour, which explains the theft.

"THE DYING SWAN

"O Silver-throated Swan
Struck, struck! A golden dart
Clean through thy breast has gone
Home to thy heart.
Thrill, thrill, O silver throat!
O silver trumpet, pour
Love for defiance back
On him who smote!
And brim, brim o'er
With love; and ruby-dye thy track
Down thy last living reach
Of river, sail the golden light—
Enter the sun's heart—even teach,
O wondrous-gifted Pain, teach thou
The god to love, let him learn how." [29] *

Defiance, love, death, pain, heart-stricken song, blood, bril-
liance—these elements in Sturge Moore's poem are all of use
to Yeats in his appropriated image. And though the swan singing before death is one of the commonest of the beast fables
or vulgar errors, it chimes so perfectly with Yeats's concep-

tion of pride that he manages to make it seem new-minted and intense.

The swan returns in that most powerfully bitter and desolating of all his poems, "Nineteen Hundred and Nineteen." The First World War is past; violence is upon the roads in Ireland, and the bloody guerrilla warfare of Black-and-Tans and Irish Republicans shows "the weasel's twist, the weasel's tooth." Imbedded in the heart of these sections devoted to mockery and destruction, the third section uses the swan again as a symbol for the artist's pride, now coupled with the idea of solitude in the face of death and approaching night.

> Some moralist or mythological poet
> Compares the solitary soul to a swan;
> I am satisfied with that,
> Satisfied if a troubled mirror show it,
> Before that brief gleam of its life be gone,
> An image of its state;
> The wings half spread for flight,
> The breast thrust out in pride
> Whether to play, or to ride
> Those winds that clamour of approaching night.

Then follows a stanza developing more directly a man's own secret meditation, his triumph and solitude, before the last stanza where the return to the swan image satisfies Yeats's bitterness at the crack-pated dream of mending the world:

> The swan has leaped into the desolate heaven:
> That image can bring wildness, bring a rage
> To end all things, to end
> What my laborious life imagined, even
> The half-imagined, the half-written page.

The image is growing in intensity and complexity, so that now, as with all of his symbols, Yeats can use it as a kind of shorthand, which will bring up for him and for "those few people who have read all that I have written" unexpressed emotions. In "Among School Children" (1928), for instance, though the swan is mentioned directly only once, it dominates in imagery three of the eight stanzas, associated with ideas of wildness and wind, of rage and pride and unsatisfied desire. Above all, the idea of a union between perfect beauty and divine strength—passion *and* conquest—in the half-expressed image of Leda and the swan. These are the shorthand fragments:

> I dream of a Ledaean body, bent
> Above a sinking fire . . .
> For even daughters of the swan can share
> Something of every paddler's heritage . . .
> And I though never of Ledaean kind
> Had pretty plumage once. . . .

The imagery is so strong that it colors and shapes other images, as in the first fragment quoted above it colors and shapes a recollection from Ronsard (which elsewhere Yeats has adapted as an entire poem [30]). Similarly, the same fragment within its own stanza impinges upon Yeats's comparison drawn from Aristophanes' fable of the separated halves of lovers seeking reunion, and unexpectedly shapes it by attraction into an image governed by the thought of the eggs from which Leda's children by Zeus were born:

> . . . it seemed that our two natures blent
> Into a sphere from youthful sympathy,
> Or else, to alter Plato's parable,
> Into the yolk and white of the one shell.

And finally, "Coole and Ballylee, 1931." The year is part of the title: Yeats is now in his late sixties. The October twilight

is gone; the season is winter and the mood is winter. The first
stanza follows the course of the stream darkening underground
as it flows from Yeats's Thoor Ballylee, where he writes the
poem, to the lake at Coole Park.

What's water but the generated soul?

In the second stanza, Yeats again is standing on that lake shore,
this time under a wintry sun; the wood is all dry sticks;
Nature is in a tragic mood that mirrors his own; then the
swan passage:

> At sudden thunder of the mounting swan
> I turned about and looked where branches break
> The glittering reaches of the flooded lake.
>
> Another emblem there! That stormy white
> But seems a concentration of the sky;
> And, like the soul, it sails into the sight
> And in the morning's gone, no man knows why;
> And is so lovely that it sets to right
> What knowledge or its lack had set awry,
> So arrogantly pure, a child might think
> It can be murdered with a spot of ink.

The succeeding stanzas meditate on Lady Gregory's house
at Coole Park. Again he can use shorthand, for in so many
of his stately reflective lyrics—"Coole Park, 1929," "Meditations in Time of Civil War," "A Prayer for My Daughter,"
"Shepherd and Goatherd," "In Memory of Major Robert
Gregory," "To a Friend Whose Work Has Come to Nothing"
—he has fingered in many modulations his worship of family,
tradition, honor, dignity, so frequently that he can assume that
a single impressionistic phrase ("a last inheritor," "ancestral
trees") will conjure up Custom and Ceremony as a refuge for

the artist, as Lady Gregory was a protection and a haven for the wracked young Yeats more than thirty years before. But in the modern world of fashion and fantasy and fanaticism, man is homeless as a Bedouin—"all that great glory spent."

Then the last stanza with its elegiac lament for tradition, beauty, the simplicity of the folk and the elevation of art, and its return to the symbol of the swan drifting upon the waters in a darkening world:

> We were the last romantics—chose for theme
> Traditional sanctity and loveliness;
> Whatever's written in what poets name
> The book of the people; whatever most can bless
> The mind of man or elevate a rhyme;
> But all is changed, that high horse riderless,
> Though mounted in that saddle Homer rode
> Where the swan drifts upon a darkening flood.

I do not wish to murder Yeats's swan with a spot of ink by glossing his lines at too great length, though it may be fair to mention that of this particular swan Yeats wrote his wife on February 3, 1932: "a symbol of inspiration I think." [31] And it is fair also to suggest that for Yeats "The Wild Swans at Coole" is but a part of a continuous experience of living, that the poignancy of that one sharp experience is increased if the reader is simultaneously aware of the similar experience reflected in part fifteen years before in "The Withering of the Boughs," and of the reenacting of the experience twelve years later in "Coole and Ballylee, 1931." Then "The Wild Swans" becomes the central portion of a three-part symphony, to which other poems also contribute auxiliary motifs.

And although the phrases come from other poems, "The Wild Swans at Coole" may be more fully realized when we know that a king and queen wandering in the sleepy country were made "happy and hopeless" by their song; that a swan sings his last song while floating out "upon a long last reach of glittering stream"; that in the proud swan, breast thrust out and wings half spread for flight, the solitary soul may see "an image of its state"; that its "feathered glory," its "white rush," "its stormy white," its "sudden thunder" as it mounts to ride the clamorous winds, its leap "into the desolate heaven"—are merely the intense poetic visions that catch its arrogant purity. Yeats's poems respond to—indeed, they compel—a knowledge of his other poems.

His symbols also presuppose or compel knowledge of their complementary or opposed symbols. The swan can be better understood if one is aware of his opposites, particularly of the phoenix and the eagle or hawk. If anyone approves of books with such titles as "Animal Imagery in Shakespeare" or "Milton's Knowledge of Horticulture," a long one could be written on birds in Yeats. It would include the peacock and the heron, the owl, the daws and the linnet, the stare or starling, bats, cattlebirds, the cock and cockerel (a long chapter), gulls (another long chapter), geese and wild geese and the barnacle goose, cuckoos, ravens, rooks, jackdaws, the peewit, the curlew, the sea-mew, lapwings, swallows, parrots, and crows. Not to mention "an absurd portly green-pated bird" on which Yeats furnishes no more specific ornithological information. The imaginary book should have a long chapter on hawks and eagles, and a long introduction on Yeatsian birds in general—particularly on his fascinated dwelling upon birdsong. The cry of birds, like his symbol of the gong or bell, seems to be an emblem of instinctive passionate unthinking life that breaks the trance of eternity.[32] * In his *Last Poems*, the birds definitely become symbols: they are not particularized, but appear as "a long-legged bird, A symbol of longevity," or "A great black ragged bird." [33] Those "bird-like things" among the shrouds end the poem "Cuchulain Comforted" on the eery line:

They had changed their throats and had the throats
    of birds.

And his last play, "The Death of Cuchulain," comes to its epilogue as the crow-headed Morrigu stands motionless upon a
slowly darkening stage: "There is silence and in the silence a
few faint bird notes."

But this chapter will not turn into a parliament of fowls,
nor will it guarantee that the roll call is complete. The design
has been merely to look for Yeats's theory of the lyric—the
cold, hard, brave, proud pattern, intense with passion, all its
strength and sweetness rolled up into one ball, not dynamic or
kinetic but static in its lyric purity. As such, the lyric is not to
be judged by criticism that insists upon standards essentially
dramatic or ironic. A poem, even a poem by Yeats, is legitimately self-contained to the extent that it should be judged, at
some point in a criticism, by its own standards—by what it is
trying to do. And Yeats is not trying to be dramatic or ironic
in the common meanings of those words. Drama and irony
would break the trancelike ecstasy Yeats tries to evoke and
maintain. His drama, such as it is, is the quarrel of a man with
himself, and he sees this not as a changing movement but as a
fixed design, like a mask, a hawk painted upon a curtain, a
bronze head, a statue, an Eastern city, a horoscope, a tower
above a stream, a six-pointed star. As for irony, his characteristic nearest approximation is in his antitheses and antinomies,
and these are in such sharp opposition that the pattern and the
effect are broken and lost if one term is taken for the other.

Nor should Yeats be judged by the literary theory of the
self-contained poem. He pours his whole personality, increasingly coherent and consistent, into every poem, so that the
poem is self-contained only in the sense that it contains all
of Yeats's own self. Nor is he a self-contained man, but a part
of all that he has met. In theory, he believed that much of his

work came even from sources over which he had no conscious control and of which he had no conscious knowledge. By a series of echoes and allusions and repetitions from poem to poem, he gave rich texture and underpainting to even his shortest lyrics. As a line from a tragedy or epic lives with added vigor because of its great context, so a lyric of Yeats gains part of its force from its being one of many related lyrics. By this device of repetition, applied with unparalleled persistence and passion, Yeats elevated the possibilities of the lyric to hitherto unrealized heights. In the history of poetry this may eventually be counted as his greatest achievement.

As a demonstration of his method, "The Wild Swans at Coole" was selected because of its surface simplicity. It has not been "analyzed," for to do so would be to defeat Yeats's intention and achievement. But the most important related material from other poems has been set forth to suggest that the swan, *though it should be experienced as an indivisible single image*, is rich in thought and complex in passion.

This, then, was the dilemma of the lyric poet: to give simultaneously the variety of actual life and the intensity of art. The multiplicity of the waters, of fish, flesh and fowl, and yet the simplicity of fire. Complexity and compression at the same time. Yeats confronted the antinomies and triumphed as an artist. All of the birds and all of the bird-songs are transmuted into the golden nightingale.

Always compression, greater and yet greater compression. No one but Yeats could have written his own epitaph. An earlier version had yet one more line which, in the cutting of this agate, Yeats finally found unnecessary:

> Cast a cold eye
> On life, on death.
> Horseman, pass by! [34]

CHAPTER FOUR

THE PURPOSE OF POETRY

"Out of the strong came forth sweetness."
—*Judges*, XIV, 14.

". . . an Ireland
The poets have imagined, terrible and gay."
—"The Municipal Gallery Revisited."

YEATS had beliefs suitable for poetry—convictions that were desires, and such as could never be imprisoned in mere opinions. His beliefs protected the life of contemplation, with its awareness of man's infinite possibilities and hopes, against the strong pressure of the life of action which gives us our statesmen, our engineers and our men of business. Furthermore, he shaped a theory of poetic symbols which, after long experiment and unremitting diligence, resulted in successful poems. He gave a new greatness to the lyric, so that in his hands it need no longer be considered a minor form of poetry, beyond or beneath criticism, the frail sister of the epic narrative and the tragic drama.

Yet what good does a poem do? Why bother with such a difficult thing at all—difficult to create, difficult to appreciate? Poetry has long been tugged by critics between its double ends of teaching and delighting. If teaching is the end, why not save energy by holding to pure philosophy or science? If delight is the end, why not avoid meaningful words and return, if we can, to the pure condition of music? Yet neither radical answer can satisfy us. We know that poetry is not written *merely* to point a moral: no one beyond the mental age of twelve should think that we have satisfactorily handled *Macbeth* by saying that it teaches how ambition is punished. On the other hand, if we feel, as most of us do, that more pleasure is derived from *Lear* than from *Atalanta in Calydon*, then in some fashion the significance of the experience must enter into the pleasure derived from a work of art.

Let us make the perpetual compromise and assume that poetry teaches *through* delighting. And let us cut corners with a further assumption: that poetry teaches by transferring from creator to reader an interpreted experience. Call it simply communication, if you will. Or presentation. Or revelation. Whatever you call it, the recreated experience of another will add to knowledge or consciousness in our own minds, and to that extent it has taught us something which we did not know before.

If we brashly take these shortcuts, we may concentrate on the question: *How* does poetry delight us? Yeats is definite as to the fact of delight. He writes: "The test of poetry is not in reason but in a delight not different from the delight that comes to a man at the first coming of love into the heart." [1] And he is as definite that delight is the artist's business when he writes of himself as a young man: "I would have a week's anxiety over the problem: do the arts make us happier, or more sensitive and therefore more unhappy. And I would say to Hughes or Sheppard, 'If I cannot be certain they make us happier I will never write again.' " [2]

How does poetry delight us? To begin with the most inclusive reason, poetry delights us as a manifestation of energy. A poem is an act, and should give us the certainty, the reflected pleasure, that comes from participating in a successful accomplishment. Yeats's bold vigor would respond easily to the aesthetic theory that art is play for play's sake.[3] * Has he not written of the poets with generous recklessness: "Our heady craft commended wasteful virtues"? [4] * Or with equal abandon, that literature now demands the right of "exploration of all that passes before the mind's eye, and merely because it passes. Yet is it not most important to explore especially what has been long forbidden, and to do this not only 'with the highest moral purpose', like the followers of Ibsen, but gaily out of sheer mischief, or sheer delight in that play of the mind?" [5] *

Poetry, as an act of creation, is an affirmation of life. "Poetry belongs to that element in every race which is most strong." [6] * Of the poet, more than of most of us, it may be said: "He would have had men live well, not merely that they might win eternal happiness but that they might live splendidly among men and be celebrated in many songs. How could one live well if one had not the joy of the Creator and of the Giver of gifts?" [7] All poets affirm living spirit of some sort, even in their most satiric and bitter denials, but some poets affirm more than others. Yeats at his most characteristic does not have the silvery opalescence, the muted tones, of his great compatriot James Joyce. His vitality is such that he praises life and art for partaking so much of each other, and looks on both "cheerfully, as one watches some handsome spirited horse." [8] * Life and art are not altogether distinguished when he writes in admiration of William Morris:

"I . . . soon discovered his spontaneity and joy and made him my chief of men. To-day I do not set his poetry very high, but for an odd altogether wonderful line, or thought; and yet, if some angel offered me the choice, I would choose to live his life, poetry and all, rather than my own or any other man's.[9] *

Artistic creation as an asseveration of life has never been phrased with more magnificence than in his sentence: "There is in the creative joy an acceptance of what life brings, because we have understood the beauty of what it brings, or a hatred of death for what it takes away, which arouses within us, through some sympathy perhaps with all other men, an energy so noble, so powerful, that we laugh aloud and mock, in the terror or the sweetness of our exaltation, at death and oblivion." [10]

Art as delight in action lies back of his analysis of J. M. Synge's development: "He had to take the first plunge into the world beyond himself, the first plunge away from himself that is always pure technique, the delight in doing, not because one would or should, but merely because one can do." [11]

But in this last quotation Yeats is already adding another element. With the pure joy of doing he is blending the joy of technique, the joy of doing a thing well or perfectly. He realized that this process demanded discipline, purification. He writes: "I have had to learn how hard, in one who lives where forms of expression and habits of thought have been born, not for the pleasure of begetting but for the public good, is that purification from insincerity, vanity, malignity, arrogance, which is the discovery of style." [12] *

The artificer's delight in his craft is evident in his preface to *The Cutting of an Agate*. His defense of a decade of work for "a small, unpopular theatre" might apply with even more force to lyric poems, which, we may assume, are even smaller and more unpopular. "This art," he writes, "may well seem to practical men . . . of no more account than the shaping of an agate; and yet in the shaping of an agate, whether in the cutting, or in the making of the design, one discovers, if one have a speculative mind, thoughts that may seem important and principles that may be applied to life itself. Certainly if one does not believe so, one is but a poor cutter of so hard a stone." [13]

When Yeats allows men "The Choice," in his memorable phrase:

> The intellect of man is forced to choose
> Perfection of the life, or of the work,[14]

the artist's choice, perfection of the work, is lower only in comparison with the beatitude of the saint. Yeats holds to this high parallel when he writes of Synge's early poems: "As yet the craftsmanship was not fine enough to bring the artist's joy which is of one substance with that of sanctity." [15] And a quarter century later he still writes: "All skill is joyful." [16] This delight in achieving perfect form requires strenuous application. However violently intractable his raw materials, as a craftsman the artist must apply himself with the deliberate diligence of the agate-cutter, the cunning of the watch-maker. His poet friends of the 'nineties, Yeats writes, "had what I still lacked, conscious deliberate craft, and what I must lack always, scholarship. They had taught me that violent energy, which is like a fire of straw, consumes in a few minutes the nervous vitality, and is useless in the arts. Our fire must burn slowly, and we must constantly turn away to think, constantly analyse what we have done, be content even to have little life outside our work, to show, perhaps, to other men, as little as the watch-mender shows, his magnifying glass caught in his screwed-up eye. Only then do we learn to conserve our vitality, to keep our mind enough under control and to make our technique sufficiently flexible for expression of the emotions of life as they arise." [17] *

The delight in perfect form demands scrupulous attention to the smallest details—of rhythm, of rhyme, of word order.[18] * Yeats knows, no less than Wordsworth, the pleasure that comes from controlled form, "the power of metre in itself," the delight which "is to be ascribed to small, but continual and regular impulses of pleasurable surprise from the metrical arrangement." [19] But perfection of the work depends not only on craftsmanship in small details, but upon style considered as a lofty controlling tension, and upon the ordering of the whole. Yeats writes with an almost Arnoldian high seriousness when he declares that a poet, though he hides nothing of himself, must speak with "a care of that dignity which should manifest itself, if not in the perfection of form, at all events with an invisible, insensible, but effectual endeavour after this lofty and severe quality, I was about to say this virtue." [20] * And though the poets desire life in their complaints and praises, they must not surrender to their emotions, but maintain a reserve, an artifice, a "deceit," which "will give us style, mastery, that dignity, that lofty and severe quality." [21] *

The perfect details, the controlling style, and above all, the organizing principle of the whole. The world of great imaginative art "must grow consistent with itself, emotion must be related to emotion by a system of ordered images, as in the *Divine Comedy*. It must grow to be symbolic, that is, for the soul can only achieve a distinct separated life where many related objects at once distinguish and arouse its energies in their fulness." [22] And with this quotation, the wheel has come full circle; we are back with delight in art springing from spiritual energy which is now realized more fully through the distinctions, the consistency, the order, of a controlled form.

Yet if art delights the will through manifest actions, and delights the intellect and the aesthetic sense through perfect form, it may also delight the emotions through giving intensity and fullness to experience. This third principle of pleasure is already brushed upon in the last quotations, where the ordering of art rouses the energies of the soul in their *fullness*.

Art in the great tradition exalts the emotions toward some ideal, some noble mood which to the practical mind seems impossible. "Every writer," Yeats declares, "even every small writer, who has belonged to the great tradition, has had his dream of an impossibly noble life, and the greater he is, the more does it seem to plunge him into some beautiful or bitter reverie." [23] This conviction makes clear the close relation in Yeats's mind between art and desire: the greater the artist, the more impossibly noble the dream, the emotion, which he creates. Again and again, Yeats in his critical meditations associates the idea of joy in art with the ideas of desire and of fullness of living.

"I thought . . . that if a powerful and benevolent spirit has shaped the destiny of this world, we can better discover that destiny from the words that have gathered up the heart's desire of the world, than from historical records, or from speculation, wherein the heart withers." [24]

". . . the kingdoms of poetry, where there is no peace that is not joyous, no battle that does not give life instead of death . . ." [25]

"We are only permitted to desire life, and all the rest should be our complaints or our praise of that exacting mistress who can awake our lips into song with her kisses." [26] And once, at least, when he wishes to proclaim a peace between Christianity and the old nature-faith which he finds so congenial to artists, Yeats gives an analysis of the joy of poetry which summarizes most of what this chapter has so far been concerned with. He finds the joy moral and almost religious. The language of poetry combines natural energy with subtle emotion, ethical intensity, and intellectual order. He writes:

"There can be no language more worthy of poetry and of the meditation of the soul than that which has been made, or can be made, out of a subtlety of desire, an emotion of sacrifice, a delight in order, that are perhaps Christian, and myths and images that mirror the energies of woods and streams, and of their wild creatures." [27]

If intensity of emotion is desirable, inasmuch as it realizes more fully man's possibilities, and if the tragic emotions are the most intense, then one may accept the final paradox that pain evoked in art may convey exaltation, ecstasy. We are led to a realization of what Yeats calls "that tragic ecstasy which is the best that art—perhaps that life—can give." The brotherhood of poets—"we artists"—serve "life in its nobler forms, where joy and sorrow are one." This, then, is the final mystery: that the exaltation of tragedy is the highest joy that art affords.[28] *

Joy through action, joy through form, joy through intensity. Will, intellect, and emotion moving together, the highest delight is joy through integration, so that the whole life of man is affirmed, pain and pleasure are no longer distinguishable in the high dream, and tragic joy is no paradox but simple truth. This is Yeats's deliberate, heartening thought in his observation on the poetic art—remarks dropped casually and never systematized. What need of a system for convictions which he had lived with his life long, which to him were as transparent and circumambient as the air he breathed?

But this is prose criticism. What of his poems? The lyrics give even better answers, for Yeats's knowledge of the purpose of poetry assumes values so exalted and tenuous that they may be experienced in poetry more acutely than they can be stated in prose.

We may give body to the airy theme by considering actual people. In his late elegiac poem "The Municipal Gallery Revisited," (1940) he recalls Griffith's pride, O'Higgins' remorseless unrest, the Venetian beauty and gentleness of an unnamed woman, Augusta Gregory's pride and humility and honor, "John Synge himself, that rooted man." Here again is the worship of life, aristocratic or rooted in the soil, the "Dream

of the noble and the beggar-man." And the proud memorial
concluded with:

> Think where man's glory most begins and ends,
> And say my glory was I had such friends.

The long lyric memorializing his friends is the type of extended
poem which Yeats writes most frequently. He turns his past
memories into present joys.

Let us begin with the Baron Von Hügel in the poem "Vacillation" (1932). There is a real separation in thought between
Yeats and that Catholic mystic, though they have some common sympathies:

> . . . for we
> Accept the miracles of the saints and honour sanctity.[29]

The way of the mystic is not the way of the poet, who images
a world, or, if he renounces it, depends still upon the world
for images of his renunciation—tangible, worldly symbols of
the ladder or the stairway by which he ascends to other ex-
istences. If the soul of a philosophical mystic may counsel:
"Seek out reality, leave things that seem," the heart of a poet
replies: "What, be a singer born and lack a theme?" The theme
for Yeats is not purification from mortality in the simplicity
of fire, but the theme of Homer: original sin.

> Homer is my example and his unchristened heart.

Yet Yeats, though he may argue with Von Hügel in his
poem—about transmigration of souls, for instance—does not
betray poetry by replacing one creed with another. The poem
itself is called "Vacillation," and its first section poses the end
of art in the form of an unanswered query:

> Between extremities
> Man runs his course;
> A brand, or flaming breath,

Comes to destroy
All those antinomies
Of day and night;
The body calls it death,
The heart remorse.
But if these be right
What is joy?

Here life is envisioned in its antinomies, and affirmed by the negation of its enemies: death for the body, remorse for the heart, since remorse destroys or wishes to destroy our own past actions. The fifth and sixth sections of this poem in eight movements repeat this negative theme, so that the intricate sunlit leafage of life is without joy for Yeats in certain moods of responsibility and remorse, and so that the glories of nature, of war, of art, may fade before that ancient melancholy theme: "Let all things pass away." Yet even this weary sixth section holds the note of revolt, of creation:

From man's blood-sodden heart are sprung
Those branches of the night and day
Where the gaudy moon is hung.

The tree imagery is developed most fully in the second section, which again emphasizes the antinomies—death and life, intellect and passion, demon and beast, "That staring fury and the blind lush leaf." [30] * Yet the man who experiences the warfare of opposites, which never concludes in a victory, though he must accept the mystery, cannot grieve. Grief is the acknowledgment of impossibilities; poetry is the discovery of possibilities. The man who is wholly conscious of his mortal manhood

May know not what he knows, but knows not grief.

Confirmed in this realization, Yeats now moves in the third section to the resolution of an artist growing old. After an ironical first stanza, he frees himself from the "Lethean foliage" of passionate or practical life; he tests every work of intellect, faith, and art and discards all those

> That are not suited for such men as come
> Proud, open-eyed and laughing to the tomb.

From this resolution, in a movement of the whole poem reminiscent of Keats's odes, the next section rises to a moment of ecstasy. Fifty years old, Yeats sits alone in a crowded London tea-shop.

> While on the shop and street I gazed
> My body of a sudden blazed;
> And twenty minutes more or less
> It seemed, so great my happiness,
> That I was blessèd and could bless.[31] *

The poet's blaze of inspiration is not Isaiah's coal, not the penitent mystic's "simplicity of fire." It is Shelley's mind in creation, which is as a fading coal. Therefore the two low-keyed fifth and sixth sections, already mentioned, now follow, though even in them we get the recoil to passion. The seventh section, in dialogue form, might suggest "Vacillation," but the Heart has the last word, and the Soul's reality and salvation seem bloodless. Then succeeds the final section addressed directly to Von Hügel. They part in sympathy, even in partial agreement. But Yeats will not accept Christianity because it affords relief, nor because it seems most welcome in the tomb. He plays a predestined part, and ends with an arrogant blessing:

> The lion and the honeycomb, what has Scripture said?
> So get you gone, Von Hügel, though with blessings
> on your head.

"Out of the strong shall come forth sweetness." Samson's riddle of the lion and the honeycomb might well serve as an image for Yeats's transmutation of life and death into art. And to carry the parallel further, Yeats is comprehensive in his acceptance: he accepts the dead lion, and the hive that the honeybees have built in the putrefying body, and the miracle that life should come from death, or sweetness from strength.

He does not reject, for instance, Christianity. In this poem, he builds what he can make use of into his own honeycomb: Isaiah, purgatory, original sin, the miracles of the saints, the undecayed body of Saint Teresa, the riddle of Samson, the blessing on Von Hügel's head. He rejects Christianity to the extent that in his eyes it rejects the world. And he will no more reject the world than he will reject spirit. Both are parts of life, which man must affirm in the teeth of death, "proud, open-eyed and laughing."

Who, then, are the strong, whom he can accept and exalt in his poetry? We might choose Lady Gregory, or Maud Gonne, or Mabel Beardsley, or John O'Leary the Fenian. But O'Leary becomes the spirit of all romantic Ireland, and Maud Gonne is transformed into a score of universal symbols. Proportion will be better maintained if we take a figure who does not touch Yeats's life in so many places, yet a figure whom he admires, and whom he builds with others into a symbol of bravery. Let us choose Lady Gregory's son. The elegy "In Memory of Major Robert Gregory" [32] is written in Yeats's most spacious style. He follows his ceremonious custom of consecrating tradition and memory by summoning up dead friends.[33] * First comes courteous Lionel Johnson who "brooded upon sanctity." Next comes John Synge, "That dying chose the living world for text," and after long travels came

> In a most desolate stony place,
> Towards nightfall upon a race
> Passionate and simple like his heart.

Then Yeats's own uncle, George Pollexfen, in his muscular youth a lover of "pure-bred horses and solid men." These men have been long dead.

> I am accustomed to their lack of breath,
> But not that my dear friend's dear son,
> Our Sidney and our perfect man,
> Could share in that discourtesy of death.

The poem is half done. The last half limns Robert Gregory, in successive stanzas devoted to his delight in the world, his horsemanship, his promise as a painter, his gift in shaping metal, wood, plaster, or stone. The poem flares up in the next-to-the-last stanza in admiration of the intensity of this man, who was, as it were, "all life's epitome"; and rounds off, again like Keats, into a framing elegiac meditation and a final heart-stopping thought.[34] *

Intensity and fullness of life are the standards. They may manifest themselves in many possible combinations. Yeats yokes them in a temporal triad:

> All those that manhood tried, or childhood loved
> Or boyish intellect approved.

Or, after two lines of natural description—

> We dreamed that a great painter had been born
> To cold Clare rock and Galway rock and thorn—

the next three lines will link aesthetic perception with intellectual order and triumphing emotion:

> To that stern colour and that delicate line
> That are our secret discipline
> Wherein the gazing heart doubles her might.

Intensity, delight, action, perfection—all enter in specifically as elements in the five-stanza ideal portrait of Robert Gregory.[35] * The portrait opens with a lover's expansive acceptance of all life:

> For all things the delighted eye now sees
> Were loved by him;

rides through a stanza of bold horsemanship; picks up centrality and power in a thrice-repeated refrain:

> Soldier, scholar, horseman, he;

and bursts in its climactic stanza into praise—and exhibition—of the flaming intensity of quintessential life:

> Some burn damp faggots, others may consume
> The entire combustible world in one small room
> As though dried straw, and if we turn about
> The bare chimney is gone black out
> Because the work had finished in that flare.
> Soldier, scholar, horseman, he,
> As 'twere all life's epitome.
> What made us dream that he could comb grey hair?

The companion-piece to this elegy "In Memory of Major Robert Gregory" is better known. It is "An Irish Airman Foresees His Death," and it, too, contains "A lonely impulse of delight." Here, also, is the self-created life—action not because of law or duty or applause, but out of high pride. There is a dispassionate withdrawal here, the cool unsentimentality that gives any of his heroes or heroines "so straight a back":[36]*

> Those that I fight I do not hate,
> Those that I guard I do not love;
> My country is Kiltartan Cross,
> My countrymen Kiltartan's poor,
> No likely end could bring them loss
> Or leave them happier than before.

The purifying and universalizing process of this lyric poet is already at work. Johnson, Synge, and Pollexfen, kindred spirits, had been used to introduce the idealized memory of their new friend in bravery and death. Now Major Robert Gregory withdraws into the less personalized Irish airman; and the airman is associated with the fisherman or the horseman, Yeats's timeless symbols for the best in Ireland and Irish history. Part of the joy that Yeats creates in his poems comes from the evocation of spirited life, either in brief recollected moments in the lives of actual people, or in such generic symbols of humanity as are best represented by his poem "The Fisherman." [37]

Persons, real or imagined, have come first in considering the delight which Yeats's poems express, for in a person the various qualities that rouse a poet's joy may be blended. But all of the joys of art which Yeats analyzes in his critical writings may be found in his poems as well—the delight in action, the delight in form, the delight in intensity, the delight in integrity.

He can find (again to take the most inclusive first) an "aimless joy" in watching birds upon a little lake—stupid happy creatures that rouse his whole nature.[38] "An aimless joy is a pure joy." [39] The old images of Homer and of the fountain blend in the uncritical worship of life:

> Yet Homer had not sung
> Had he not found it certain beyond dreams
> That out of life's own self-delight had sprung
> The abounding glittering jet.[40]

The proud stretching toward perfection, the artist's keeping himself at strain until he conquers, comes out when Yeats cries that for his imagined Irish fisherman:

> Before I am old
> I shall have written him one
> Poem maybe as cold
> And passionate as the dawn.[41]

And in *Last Poems* the joy and triumph in perfect artistry is
expressed over and over:

> Let the fools rage, I swerved in nought,
> Something to perfection brought.
> —"What Then?"

In "Under Ben Bulben," dated September 4, 1938, Yeats at the
age of seventy-three leaves as a legacy to artists the ideal of
strenuous craftsmanship:

> Poet and sculptor, do the work, . . .
> Bring the soul of man to God.

> . . . there's a purpose set
> Before the secret working mind:
> Profane perfection of mankind.

> Irish poets, learn your trade,
> Sing whatever is well made. . . .
> Sing the peasantry, and then
> Hard-riding country gentlemen,
> The holiness of monks, and after
> Porter-drinkers' randy laughter;
> Sing the lords and ladies gay
> That were beaten into the clay
> Through seven heroic centuries;
> Cast your mind on other days
> That we in coming days may be
> Still the indomitable Irishry.

The idea of joy derived from art through the sheer intensity of the passion expressed is exemplified on every page of Yeats. Lines such as

By that great glory driven wild [42]

are so characteristic that this notion of intensity could be best exemplified by quoting in full all of his poems during his great period.

More difficult to follow is the idea of joy through integrated life. Such integration can come only with age. In "Demon and Beast," published when Yeats was in his middle fifties, laughing freedom is won through the reconciliation of opposites.[43] Though only the passion of intellect or the passion of youth may attain "right mastery of natural things," nevertheless the artist's mere growing old may bring the sweetness of the clear-eyed freeman. Twelve years later, the quarrel of a man with himself is again resumed in "A Dialogue of Self and Soul." [44] The Soul speaks in terms of the cyclical recurrence of life in history or the individual. Ancestral night can deliver us from the crime of death and birth. But the Self bravely answers and claims the soldier's right to commit the crime of generation again. In the last half of the poem the Soul is quiet, while the Self acknowledges the blindness, impurity, toil, ignominy, distress, pain, and clumsiness of life. It acknowledges that society may give any man a "defiling and disfigured shape." It dares to describe living as pitching into

the frog-spawn of a blind man's ditch,
A blind man battering blind men;

and to touch upon the heart-mystery of Yeats's own spiritual agony. Yet the Self accepts life, and is content to live it all again and yet again. With this acceptance, this integration, the poem can end:

When such as I cast out remorse
So great a sweetness flows into the breast
We must laugh and we must sing,
We are blest by everything,
Everything we look upon is blest.[45] *

Again we have the miracle—for paradox is too small a word
—that from the positive acceptance of *all* life, including its
defilement and folly, may flow sweetness, laughter, singing,
even blessedness. Here Yeats is not far from Shakespeare's
thought in his later tragedies and his last romances.[46] * More
than one poem in the volume of *Last Poems* returns to this
great theme of the old artist setting his lands in order, for what
peace and joy such comprehensive clarity may afford him.

The most obvious antinomy in this integration into a final
joy is the opposition between personal pain and impersonal
joyous art. Here again is the mystery of tragedy, that

> Out of cavern comes a voice,
> And all it knows is that one word 'Rejoice!'

that

> We that look on but laugh in tragic joy;

that even the unthinking people demand

> A laughing, crying, sacred song;

that the Ireland the poets have imagined is "terrible and gay." [47]
Only hysterical women think that in a sad world artists should
not be gay. Perhaps Nero's one commendable accomplishment was that he fiddled while Rome burned. Some fiddler
should always remind us that no catastrophe is final. And if
the world, or we, were to end tomorrow, so much the more
reason to affirm intense life today.

> All perform their tragic play,
> There struts Hamlet, there is Lear,
> That's Ophelia, that Cordelia;
> Yet they, should the last scene be there,
> The great stage curtain about to drop,
> If worthy their prominent part in the play,
> Do not break up their lines to weep.
> They know that Hamlet and Lear are gay;
> Gaiety transfiguring all that dread.[48] *

Only so may we find "Tragedy wrought to its uttermost." To the whole man—who is not only tragic but joyful—death and birth are not crimes but accepted mysteries. He knows that

> All things fall and are built again,
> And those that build them again are gay.

The final joy of the artist is creation, and the greatness of his creation will depend upon the completeness with which he embraces and accepts all materials. Yeats is of the Renaissance in his belief in the poet as a creator, comparable only to his heavenly maker.[49] * The intensity of the poet as self-creator he has nowhere expressed with more of the poet's intensity than in his burning lines:

> Whatever flames upon the night
> Man's own resinous heart has fed.[50]

The profound secret of this positive act of creation lies in tragedy itself. The tragic spirit might be defined as the simultaneous awareness of man's limitations and of his infinite capabilities. The poet, with his desire for perfection, knows man's possibilities, the ideals toward which he so haltingly strives. The poet, with his consciousness of the actual and individual world, knows no less man's limitations. The source of art may well be some actual limitation, some imperfection, some aching void, some agony, that demands in answer the poet's created affirmation of the ideal or the possible. Too frequently to be accidental, Yeats suggests that his poems spring from an irritation, an emptiness, or a wound.[51] * The typical movement may be seen in a letter Yeats writes in his seventy-second year:

"I am far away from everybody & everything. . . . Part of my sense of solitude was that I felt I would never know that supreme experience of life—that I think possible to the young —to share profound thought & then to touch. I have come out of that darkness a man you have never known—a man of genius, more gay, more miserable." [52] The gaiety of genius grows from solitude and miserable deprivation. Man's unsatisfied soul demands satisfaction, and satisfaction is given in the joy of art.

If it is true that

> only an aching heart
> Conceives a changeless work of art,[53]

it is also true that the changeless work of art is no longer its original conception, but has been transmuted into a thing of joy.[54] * "I think," writes Yeats, quoting an early diary of his own, "all happiness depends on the energy to assume the mask of some other life." [55] One might hazard the principle that if the joy comes from the sheer act of creation, then the more painful or hopeless or personal or sordid the original materials are, the more joyful is the successful impersonal ordering— since it represents a greater triumph, the harmonizing of a greater tension and separation between first matter and final form.

Lust and rage, therefore, may spur Yeats into song. Hector may be dead and Troy burning. Numb nightmare may ride on top. "What matter?" [56] The little superficial things—flies and moths and knaves and dolts—are given their significance by the generating artist.[57] The vision of the artist may be so powerful that he may

> when it's vanished still declare,
> With only bed and bedstead there,
> That heavens had opened.[58]

Art, then, may afford joy through free creation when life is found to be too limited. As such, art becomes an alternative mode of life, deliberately willed and constructed. It is a New Jerusalem built out of old bricks near at hand. It is a golden nightingale, more glistening in color and lasting in song than its living model, whom the artificer at once complains of and praises. Art may be a substitute, so that if life had been more malleable, the poet says,

> I might have thrown poor words away
> And been content to live.[59]

But life not being malleable enough, the artist must choose perfection of the work. Frustration and fear and bitterness and indifference shake him, and he must therefore turn for certainty to poor words:

> Whereon I wrote and wrought,
> And now, being grey,
> I dream that I have brought
> To such a pitch my thought
> That coming time can say,
> 'He shadowed in a glass
> What thing her body was.' [60]

If the theme of creative joy has been too positively stated to this point in the chapter, Yeats's humor and irony and sense of reality should temper any easy optimism. A tragic joy is no thoughtless rapture. The golden nightingale is created out of the desire to capture the living nightingale. The singing school of the soul springs from impossible desire for the country which is no country for old men. The source of art, which remolds the world nearer to the heart's desire, is nowhere better shown than in that late poem "The Circus Animals' Desertion," [61] in which Yeats passes his career in review. The first section is self-criticism: he cannot in old age find a theme; he must be satisfied with his heart; he acknowledges that his past works were shows, masks, symbols—his own answers to a world that had stung him alive:

> Winter and summer till old age began
> My circus animals were all on show,
> Those stilted boys, that burnished chariot,
> Lion and woman and the Lord knows what.

The second section surveys his poetic life in three stanzas. In the first stanza he tells over the wanderings of Oisin, through three allegorical islands that represent

> Vain gaiety, vain battle, vain repose.

We may long have felt that Oisin is but a symbol for Yeats himself, but now we know it, for the enchanted islands are but "Themes of the embittered heart"; and Yeats, "starved for the bosom of his faery bride," himself set on his heroes to ride the sea-horses or to fight the invulnerable tide.

The second stanza of this middle section tells of his play *The Countess Cathleen*, in which the heroine out of pity sells her soul to the devil to save the starving Irish people. Why did he write this play? As an ideal answer to those who thought

Ireland might be saved by fanaticism and hatred of the English. Actual fanaticism is replaced by the counter-truth in art: bravery inspired by love.

> I thought my dear must her own soul destroy,
> So did fanaticism and hate enslave it,
> And this brought forth a dream and soon enough
> This dream itself had all my thought and love.[62] *

The concluding stanza of this section refers principally to his play *On Baile's Strand*. Since it deals with "Heart-mysteries," I shall not try to pluck them out, further than to suggest that the cunning middle-class Irish and their political hatreds are glanced at in the Fool and Blind Man, and that Cuchulain now seems to be the symbol for Yeats himself, and his career is the course that any lover of Ireland may take to express his love. At any rate, Yeats in this section has reviewed his maturity, has shown how personal and political issues roused him to poetry, how in the Irish Theatre movement he went here and there and made himself a motley to the view, how in a sense he was sidetracked by the painted stage and the courtly shows. Above all, he gives the theory of his theatre—a quintessential action rooted in the past and shaping the future of Ireland:

> Character isolated by a deed
> To engross the present and dominate memory.

And now the circus animals have deserted him. He had lifted them up into the unchanging realm of art, the enchanting dream, and he knows that the powerful symbols, long felt and long thought out, had become pure and solid and permanent. But where had they come from? Dare he admit their source? Dare he acknowledge that aspiration or desire solely prompts the poet's trick of transmutation? Is this "broken man" only an old disillusioned alchemist, a lion tamer without any lions? Here is the final stanza:

> Those masterful images because complete
> Grew in pure mind, but out of what began?
> A mound of refuse or the sweepings of a street,
> Old kettles, old bottles, and a broken can,
> Old iron, old bones, old rags, that raving slut
> Who keeps the till. Now that my ladder's gone,
> I must lie down where all the ladders start,
> In the foul rag-and-bone shop of the heart.

His answer could not be more uncompromising. And we are back at that peculiar quality of his beliefs which he shapes in his poems into joy. Earlier I have called it "courage." The word is not good enough. The quality Yeats admires includes physical and spiritual courage, but much more. There is also sheer pride, the ceremonious awareness of one's own personal dignity and worth, whether one is fool, beggar, or blind man. There is a vitalistic philosophy which scorns any limited system —be it science, rationalism, materialism, or any religious creed including Christianity—as being abstract. Discrimination must draw a line, and if the line is drawn in order to rule out any area of life, then it is a line of death and remorse; the unpardonable sin, in Yeats's thought, is committed, and life denies itself.

No; we must have instead integrity, acceptance, affirmation; we must have the inclusion of opposites, the wedding of antinomies, what Robert Frost calls the "lover's quarrel with the world." Crazy Jane and the beggar, the hawk and the butterfly, Solomon and the "raving slut who keeps the till" are all parts of the story. For life, as in Plato's parable, generation between Plenty and Penury is needful.

And for poetry, the quality of bravery is also needful. It will show itself in an inclusiveness in creation, which is but another word for love, as exclusiveness and abstraction are but other words for hatred.[63] * Knowing this secret in a naughty world, the artist (or the soul, or the growing child) knows joy:

> Considering that, all hatred driven hence,
> The soul recovers radical innocence
> And learns at last that it is self-delighting,
> Self-appeasing, self-affrighting,
> And that its own sweet will is Heaven's will;
> She can, though every face should scowl
> And every windy quarter howl
> Or every bellows burst, be happy still.[64]

Forgetting for a moment that this idea of spirit as the sole creator is shared with him by Plato and Plotinus, and using them merely as emblems of abstraction, Yeats declares his "faith":

> I mock Plotinus' thought
> And cry in Plato's teeth,
> Death and life were not
> Till man made up the whole,
> Made lock, stock and barrel
> Out of his bitter soul,
> Aye, sun and moon and star, all,
> And further add to that
> That, being dead, we rise,
> Dream and so create
> Translunar Paradise.[65]

Paradise out of bitterness, through man's own act of creation. In one sense, Yeats's most profound symbol is his own body of poetry. Art is perhaps the most perfect emblem for life, for it creates out of inert matter and undirected motion an individual organism with parts and a purpose.

This chapter began by following one of two roads—the road of delight as the end of art. One final word about the road not taken: instruction as the end of art. I shall not fall into Yeats's abhorred abstractions by setting up the moral beliefs that are present in almost every line quoted so far to illustrate quite different tenets. But the poet's world is inescapably a moral world, and Yeats's striving in art for joy is a moral end, which might be dignified—or would it be made trivial?—by calling it hedonism. The belief in bravery, which creates "the abounding glittering jet" of Yeats's poetry, is likewise a moral belief, to which we might give the name of stoicism, were it not set afire by so much passion.

This moral aspect of the belief in bravery needs further emphasis. Let us take it out of the frame of the critical essay because, as people think too rightly, the essay has so little to do with our mere living. While I was writing this section, I had lunch in a drugstore where by accident I met one of America's best humanists at a soda-fountain. We talked about subjects as important as you can discuss when you meet someone you respect, by accident, over a cup of coffee and a ham sandwich. He brought up a point which he must have remembered for at least two and a half years (important conversations can be quite long), disagreeing with some verses of mine in which I had attacked modern rationalistic philosophers. He said that truly current philosophy believed the world irrational —brute fact. He maintained that the science of the last three hundred years—the dispassionate, if you will the dehumanized, observation of experience—was responsible for present desperation. This is all old stuff. And then, coming from a philosopher whom I had always considered a qualified idealist, he dropped the bomb. He said that he thought science was right.

He said that science had observed the truth. He said that the experiment of man would come to an end.

I mention this as a concrete particular, at the highest level terrifying to the spirit. And I mention it entirely outside the sphere of any religious answer which might be set down in any creed. It would be an impossible position for Yeats to hold, or for any typical artist. Art, by virtue of its being art, believes in creation, not in negation. If the utter destruction of mankind were assured, then, to the edge of annihilation, the Yeatsian artist lives in joy and laughs into the face of death. If, among our innumerable "ifs," destruction is *not* assured, then the artist, still believing in creation, knows that

> All things fall and are built again,
> And those that build them again are gay.

While man remains man, poetry acts as a moral agent by constantly asserting man's own fullest nature—his complete, conscious, individual livingness. The asseveration of life in this sense belongs only to art—not to science, or philosophy, or society, or sport, or even to the day's affairs.

But let a poet speak for a poet, in the last section of W. H. Auden's "In Memory of W. B. Yeats." [66] If there are moral judgments implicit here, if the question of the purpose of poetry is again answered, then at least it is answered where the accent should be unmistakable and authentic, in poetry itself:

> Earth, receive an honoured guest;
> William Yeats is laid to rest:
> Let the Irish vessel lie
> Emptied of its poetry. . . .
>
> Follow, poet, follow right
> To the bottom of the night,
> With your unconstraining voice
> Still persuade us to rejoice;

With the farming of a verse
Make a vineyard of the curse,
Sing of human unsuccess
In a rapture of distress;

In the deserts of the heart
Let the healing fountain start,
In the prison of his days
Teach the free man how to praise.

CHAPTER FIVE

THE PROGRESS OF A POET

"We must labour to be beautiful."
—"Adam's Curse."

"Amis, qu'est-ce qu'une grande vie, sinon une
pensée de la jeunesse exécutée par l'âge mûr."
—Alfred de Vigny.

THIS final chapter plans to tell what this book is not trying
to do and then to tell what this book has tried to do.

In most books, therefore, it would appear as an introduction.
But introductions, in social life, are nuisances: they keep the
talk from flowing. Perhaps they are nuisances in little critical
volumes; certainly they are menaces. If they successfully simplify the main argument, they give readers the impression that
the rest of the book is unnecessary. Tucked away like an ap-
pendix at the end of the volume, the introduction may do less
harm, and may protect Yeats against wrong emphases and
guard the proportions of this particular study.

First of all, these interrelated chapters are not meant to be
a complete survey of Yeats as a lyric poet. They merely consider a few selected principles of poetry as exemplified in the
lyrics of William Butler Yeats. None of the principles is
exclusive of other principles; each might lead to different con-
clusions if applied to other poets. It would be possible to write
a single essay holding that the essence of Yeats is his belief in

free spirit.[1] Yet such an embracing and governing idea is suggested in this book only by implication. I believe that a book purporting to cover Yeats's poetic achievement completely is a mistake, for it would suggest that something has been done that cannot be done, setting limits to that which is inexhaustible. The mystery of art, the unpredictability of genius, should always receive some kind of acknowledgment in what is meant as faithful criticism, if for no other reason than to distinguish art from criticism. Something indescribable should be left, beyond the reach of the critic.

Many of the separate ideas referred to in the preceding essays could easily grow into chapters; any of the chapters might be expanded into a book. Yeats's philosophical clarity and artistic consistency should make technical studies relatively easy. His respect for tradition would make a good starting-point for a survey of his metrical and stanzaic forms. His purposeful ambiguity warrants a chapter. His masterful rhythms, balancing between freedom and control, are often the hidden causes of his effects. This very chapter on "The Progress of a Poet" might be technically illustrated by considering the changes that he made in phrasing, even within published versions of the same poem or drama. A comparison of the earlier states of "Sailing to Byzantium," for instance, overdecorated and relatively formless, with the final poem should convince any careful reader that the shaping of an imaginative poem is an intellectual triumph of the highest order.

Yeats offers unusually good material to see how ideas and emotions control form, or in the other direction, how form gives outline to ideas and emotions. And when that game is played, one learns again that in good art, form and content are but aspects of a single activity. Do his symbols of the fisherman, the horseman, and the hawk give greater clarity and energy to his arrogance? Or does his pride summon up the suitable symbols? Is his growing use of beggars and madmen and blind men in his later poems to be explained by his conviction of unappeasable desire? Is Yeats's craftsmanship the reaction of the Creative Mind upon the Body of Fate—that intractable world of fact that confronts the shaping imagination of every artist? Or does the world of particular facts in which each man lives compel an artist to select certain parts of his own limited experience, as a magician forces a determined playing-card upon a spectator under the illusion that choice is free? Again, a chapter on Yeats's incredibly cunning and effective sexual images might be based on his governing idea of generation, of "begetting and birth, for all things are a single form which has divided and multiplied in time and space."

This book might have been much the same in effect with an entirely different set of chapters: one on the polarity between his beliefs in intensity and eternity; one on the slow growth of his conservatism; one on his technique as it is often talked about directly in the lyrics themselves; one on his repeated uses of the words "symbol," "image," and "emblem" throughout his poems; one on the development of a completely different set of symbols, such as cloths and the sword, or the hare, or the rose, or the thorn-tree.

But the best unwritten book on Yeats as a constructor of lyrics will organize his great armies of opposing symbols into their regiments and battalions and camp-followers, and will show how they are marshaled in battle array for the engagement of each particular poem. It will be a book both of strategy and tactics. And again it will show that significant form springs alone from the clashing of powerful and noble convictions.

So much for the books that might have been written to serve purposes somewhat similar to those which control this present volume. Now for the books it could not or did not want to be. It cannot, unfortunately, be a book of personal reminiscences, though the more we have of them the better. It is not a critical study relating his accomplishments to his life. It introduces no new materials from Yeats's fascinating letters when they talk about himself and his work. It is not a collection of tributes in memory of W. B. Yeats from those who knew him or were influenced by him. It is not an informal and personal estimate of a poet by a poet. And thanks to Joseph Hone, it need not be a biography. All these books already exist.[2] It has disregarded biography and secondary sources and has concentrated on Yeats's own writings. Even here, it has been selective rather than exhaustive. Yeats's thought is so much of a piece that it would merely make the book heavy to include all of his variations on his central ideas. At the risk of some heaviness even as it is, I have tried to give enough quotations, relegating some of them to supplementary notes, and drawing them usually from various periods in his career, to show that the themes considered are central and continuing, and not casual fancies.

Even among his own writings, I have held in the main to his critical essays and to the lyric poems of his artistic maturity. Without straying from a prime interest in his lyrics, it would have been possible to consider his short stories and his plays for the light they shed upon his major interests. Furthermore, this is not a book on the lyric considered as the expression of limited highly personal emotion. A good book might be written on Yeats as a love poet. He makes every love poet since Donne and Shakespeare look bloodless and conventional in comparison, with the possible exceptions of a few poets in a few moments. But though his love poems are particularized and intense realizations, their drive is from frustration toward some understandable and permanent pattern of passion. Rossetti has said that the sonnet is

> a moment's monument,
> Memorial from the soul's eternity
> To one dead deathless hour.

Yeats's love poems are not monuments to a moment, but to the soul's eternity. They transcend, or try to transcend, any hour, whether it is dead or deathless.

The last book which this is not is a study of Yeats as satirist. The Romans would have understood him, Martial as well as Catullus. And we might include political philosophers or historians such as Tacitus and Plutarch. The crucial point in such a book would have been the nice balancing of a lyric poet on the verge of action and politics—National Theatres and Municipal Galleries and Free States and the fanatic Irish heart as materials for poems, until we are given the wry picture of the lyric poet as an Irish Senator inspecting schools (Matthew Arnold would also have laughed in satirical sympathy): "A sixty-year-old smiling public man," "a comfortable kind of old scarecrow." [3] Yeats's sense of humor and arrogance in hatred made him excelling as a satirist.[4] *

These untouched regions of Yeats's art suggest that a short sketch of his development might here be given, in order to frame the earlier chapters, as a practical aid to those unfamiliar with Yeats's work as a whole. Others may safely skip the succeeding paragraphs, since such a brief survey can only indicate an approach. The dating of any period is only approximate, for artists may live in several states at once, working over earlier themes in the heart of new interests, or experimentally scenting the faint wind from some country into which they have not yet set foot.

When in late life he came to collect, revise, and assign arbitrary dates to his poems, Yeats gives to the first grouping of his early work the title *Crossways* (1889), which suggests well enough his vacillation. *Fin de siècle* is upon him; he tries to combine the medieval tapestries of William Morris with Rossetti's wavering rhythms of the sorrowful heart. Most of the poems in this section, as he remembers them, must have been

written before he was twenty. He tried his hand at sad shep-
herds, and dim Tennysonian seas, and the cloak, boat, and
shoes of Sorrow; he went to the Orient for the exotic and the
erotic and the soulful, choosing there one theme to which he
returned more than a half century later.[5] * Yet when he started
writing his long narrative poem on the wanderings of Oisin,
his subject matter became Irish. And here again he vacillates
between the battle-cars of ancient Irish heroes, and folk-tales
from his own County Sligo, and imitation ballads.

The next section, *The Rose* (1893), deserts the folk for the
soul, and lives in a high ecstasy of mournfulness, where fog
is often mistaken for profundity. Here the fairies are the best
philosophers, and dreams are also sooth. This is the volume that
contains "The Lake Isle of Innisfree," and Yeats holds himself
ready to arise and go now wherever he may find Druids or
white birds or the rose upon the rood of time. The poems included in *The Rose* were written at about the time of his first
two plays, *The Countess Cathleen* (1892) and *The Land of
Heart's Desire* (1894). Both of these plays deal with Christian
Irish material, but a proud pagan gesture of self-sacrifice
dominates one, and the joyous dancing fairies win in the other.
It is a young man's collection, *The Rose*, dedicated to Lionel
Johnson with an epigraph from Augustine—"Too late I have
loved thee, O Beauty at once so ancient and so young!"—
and closing with a dedication of himself "To Ireland in the
Coming Times":

> Know, that I would accounted be
> True brother of a company
> That sang, to sweeten Ireland's wrong.

Shall he devote himself to beauty or to Irish salvation? Or may
he show that beauty and Ireland are one and the same? It seems
easy at times, in his amorphous youthful thought where everything may be turned—and is turned—into a Rose. But the last

poem shows some uneasiness, and is almost an apology for writing Druid tunes of elemental creatures in order to help the dim coming times.

The two decades that follow were largely given over to positive action in the cause of the Abbey Theatre. His own works for the stage tried to give the Irish a pride and a consciousness of their racial existence through summoning up heroic dreams of their past history. The plays were too heroic and too dreamy. He thought of the folk—peasants' houses and tramps and poor old women—but he pleased only the select few. Though it may be true that without Yeats there would have been no Irish theatre, no movement so organized and influential that it could come to be known as the Irish Renaissance, nevertheless the towering idealism of his ambition, the indifference of the general public, and the lack of dramatic skill in his own work, combined in a steady drift of disillusionment that increasingly moves in his lyric poems.

The Wind among the Reeds (1899) continues to blow from far countries, where the lover may reprove the curlew for crying, and hope that Ireland's enemies may be routed in the Valley of the Black Pig, and plead with Elemental Powers. The lover is very moody and very mournful, and has many wishes; and his desires, when they are not incoherent, are unappeasable. His beloved lady has pearl-pale hands and red lips, and must appear a great deal like Rossetti's *Beata Beatrix*, looking through half-closed eyelids at the same mysterious woods. Nothing seems to move through these thick twilights and dreams and dim half-lights—except the wind, which, like the birds and the lover, cries too. We are still in the woods *In the Seven Woods* (1904), and we are not out of them in *The Green Helmet and Other Poems* (1910), where lyric poetry is so much disregarded that the volume takes its name from Yeats's not very successful attempt to write "An Heroic Farce." It is as heroic as Cuchulain and Yeats can make it, but they are not the ones to make it a farce. Max Beerbohm would need to do a minimum of retouching to make it excellently farcical.

Yet this last volume shows what lies ahead. Yeats is giving up some of his parochial and antiquarian mystifications which demand an Irish library and a mind-reader for explanation. Red Hanrahan and Clooth-na-Bare are replaced by more accessible references to Homer and to Troy. The curses of frustrated love and of frustrated action in the theatre are beginning to fall away. Yeats starts to develop a cool confidence in himself. He is no longer either the mournful lover or the savior of Ireland— or at least, not all the time. He discards the "kings, Helmets, and swords, and half-forgotten things" [6] that trembled in veiled forms between himself and the real world. His power of self-analysis grows clearer, and he writes poems for the first time about his conscious art. He is still youthful enough to be sure that his youth was full of lying days, and to take a jaunty fare-well to those days, now that he is a bare ruined choir of forty-five, in the line: "Now I may wither into the truth." [7] But he is confident enough in his own powers to scorn his imitators: "Was there ever dog that praised his fleas?" [8] * And he writes little occasional poems, that Deirdre and Cuchulain might not have understood, on the world around him—the uproar against immoral literature, the land agitation, the Abbey Theatre. He is well out of the seven woods when he can write of himself:

> All things can tempt me from this craft of verse:
> One time it was a woman's face, or worse—
> The seeming needs of my fool-driven land;
> Now nothing but comes readier to the hand
> Than this accustomed toil.[9]

For the first time Yeats is hard-headedly self-conscious.

In the next twenty or twenty-five years his powers are sure and full. A reader will not have missed much, except the pious pleasure of knowing all there is to know about a friend, if he begins his reading with *Responsibilities* (1914) and carries on through the five volumes that follow. Now Yeats assumes full responsibility for his action and thought. His occasional poems on Ireland are savage, direct, powerful, immediate, slashing like lightning-strokes. His beggar ballads and songs sing recklessly and merrily. A new tension and a new liberality lift his verses; *insouciance* combines with control; the reins seem careless on the neck of a powerful thoroughbred. The symbols stand out sure, cut cleanly away from blurring dreams and draperies, and for the first time they have the characteristic Yeatsian power and move with an inexpressible life of their own. But principally *Responsibilities* is less a sample of things to come than a declaration of independence. The poems on contemporary Dublin were written in 1912–13 as "Poems Written in Discouragement," [10] yet it is not the discouragement that is evident, it is the biting scorn. The "Introductory Rhyme" shoulders his past, and begs pardon of his fierce ancestors

> that for a barren passion's sake,
> Although I have come close on forty-nine,
> I have no child, I have nothing but a book,
> Nothing but that to prove your blood and mine.

The last poem throws away his old embroidered style—like the converted Francis of Assisi casting off his youthful princely garments—for the greater enterprise of walking naked. And the "Closing Rhyme" defends his friends, his art, and ancient ceremony, against the "fling of the dull ass's hoof." The attacks of former friends, the praise of fools, the marriage of Maud Gonne in 1903, and the fanatic stupidity of old Paudeens have at last goaded him into a reckoning. He charts his past course, takes his present position, sets the wheel toward the future. But the past has not been useless, nor is it rejected completely. He builds "perfection of the life" *and* of the work from his own past failures. The last decades may seem to have been dedicated to "a barren passion," to "the blind and ignorant town," and to dreams of old queens and heroes. But he knows, and puts it as epigraph to the book, that "In dreams begins responsibility."

If the supernatural directors that were so soon to give him the materials from which he constructed his *A Vision* really existed, they are to be congratulated on having chosen so fitting an instrument as Yeats: many of the ideas shaped formally in his philosophical system may be seen half-formed and half-guessed in his earlier lyrics; and in the poems of the next volumes the rigid system serves as the ground out of which flower his most perfect works of art. Of certain of the poems [11] he writes: "To some extent I wrote these poems as a text for exposition." All of the great poems are bound to each other by innumerable subtle threads; all can be better understood with his prose writings as groundwork; yet none of them, not even among the three that form a text for exposition, is so recondite that it cannot impart some of its beauty and its thought if read separately. "They take their place," he writes, "in a phantasmagoria in which I endeavour to explain my philosophy of life and death." [12]

The historian Arnold Toynbee's theory of "withdrawal and return" fits a study of Yeats's development even more incontrovertibly than it does a study of history. Toynbee writes of "the course which is followed by creative personalities when they are taking the mystic path which is their highest spiritual level. We have seen that they pass first out of action into ecstasy and then out of ecstasy into action on a new and higher plane. . . . The withdrawal makes it possible for the personality to realize powers within himself which might have remained dormant if he had not been released for the time being from his social toils and trammels. Such a withdrawal may be a voluntary action on his part or it may be forced upon him by circumstances beyond his control; . . . but a transfiguration in solitude can have no purpose, and perhaps even no meaning, except as a prelude to the return of the transfigured personality into the social milieu out of which he had originally come: . . . The return is the essence of the whole movement as well as its final cause." [13] *

Yeats withdrew into the world of *A Vision*—formally on the afternoon of October 24, 1917. The woman, the theatre, the Ireland he loved had all proved intractable; they had gone on paths where he would not follow. His desires to be understood and to elevate through sympathy had apparently failed. He withdraws into his own lonely world,[14] * and he returns in the poems of his four finest volumes. This is merely a spiritual history of the years, roughly, 1910–1930. In the world of the greasy till, he marries happily and has children, he continues to write smaller and smaller plays for smaller and smaller audiences, and he takes a dutiful part in the new Irish State of which he cannot totally approve. But we are talking here of Yeats as an artist.

The four volumes that follow are so satisfying and maintain such a high level that there is little point in distinguishing among them. They are *The Wild Swans at Coole* (1919), *Michael Robartes and the Dancer* (1921), *The Tower* (1928), and *The Winding Stair and Other Poems* (1933). One could point out that the first two are close to *A Vision* and often assume thought which is not common. Or that the second volume is the slightest of the quartette. Or that intransigence increases through the four. Future times, no doubt, will make a game of these volumes, placing this one first for profundity, and that for sheer singing, and the other for richness of imagery, and still another for rhythmical mastery, as one plays with the Golden Comedies or the tragedies of Shakespeare.

If a guide is supposed to do more than say "Eccolo!" or "Quattrocento," then perhaps the best service is to point out the channels in which Yeats's thought most frequently runs. Each volume is the complete man; it includes Yeats in all his styles; his powers as a lyric poet are more diversified than are those of Herbert or Keats or Housman or (to take two of his own chief idols) Shelley or Blake. Classification by type is the lowest form of academic industry, and perhaps the most sinister —since its tendency is always away from the particulars of art toward the genera of science or philosophy. But classification may aid in a first encounter with a bewildering variety, just as Linnaeus may help us to set botany straight, provided always that we still enjoy the flowers and do not fall into the delusion that they were made in order to give Linnaeus something to do.

The noblest class among Yeats's poems is the long lyric in meditative or elegiac mood, still presenting a phantasmagoria for life and death. To this group belong "The Wild Swans at Coole," "In Memory of Major Robert Gregory," "Shepherd and Goatherd," "A Prayer for My Daughter," "Among School Children," "All Souls' Night," "Coole Park, 1929," and "Coole and Ballylee, 1931."

Closely associated with this group is the long symbolic poem, where the symbols in tensely ordered patterns gesture and resound beyond the reach of words. Here might be placed "Ego Dominus Tuus," "The Phases of the Moon," "The Double Vision of Michael Robartes," "Michael Robartes and the Dancers," "Sailing to Byzantium," "A Dialogue of Self and Soul," "Blood and the Moon," and "Byzantium."

Then there are the shorter lyrics, small sleeping bombs of pure uranium, built around a single symbol: "The Cat and the Moon," "The Saint and the Hunchback," "Another Song of a Fool," "Demon and Beast," "The Second Coming," "A Meditation in Time of War," "Two Songs from a Play [The Resurrection]," "Leda and the Swan," "Oil and Blood," "Symbols," "Veronica's Napkin," and "The Crazed Moon."

Some of the balancing titles in this last group suggest a form that Yeats naturally falls into to express his antinomies and oppositions: the dialogue or debate, formal or implied. Here we shall find such poems as "The Hawk," "The People," "Ego Dominus Tuus," "The Phases of the Moon," "An Image from a Past Life," "Owen Aherne and His Dancers," "A Dialogue of Self and Soul," and part of "Vacillation."

But we are already getting into trouble. Some of our poems fall into more than one class, and the classes are not water-tight. "Among School Children" is not only meditative but is symbolic in Yeats's specialized uses of symbols. "Ego Dominus Tuus" is not only symbolic but is in the form of a dialogue. And how shall we classify such a poem of the first water as "Solomon and the Witch," which is neither "short" nor "long," which depends on Yeatsian symbolism, and which is in the form of a dialogue? How ought Yeats's scholars, who "cough in ink," to classify "The Fisherman"? Instead of answering the question, let us get into further trouble.

Yeats himself thinks of his poems as related, if not classified. His lyrical spontaneity frequently wars with his philosophic coherence. It is as if Herrick were to write Lucretius. Just as Tennyson conveys a narrative in *Maud* without abandoning his lyric gifts, so Yeats builds up a single theme, a pattern, a continuity of emotion, by grouping lyrics. Some of his most beautiful larger effects are secured in this manner, and one does not know whether to compare them to chamber music, or delicate symphonies, or variations upon a theme. Here should be mentioned "Upon a Dying Lady," "The Tower," "Meditations in Time of Civil War," "Nineteen Hundred and Nineteen," "A Man Young and Old," "Blood and the Moon" and "Vacillation" again, and (though he does not group them under a single title) the five political poems beginning with "Easter, 1916." [15]

There are also the smaller categories: the quick sketches that catch a quirk of the mind and are all style and spirit in a few words; the memories too evanescent to call forth a formal elegy; the gifts (almost the apologies) to those closest to him; the aimless joy of the pure songs of jailbirds and fools; the tributes and the sharp darts; the succinct rounded Delphic utterances which close infinity in a quatrain. All of them are shot through with a gaiety and a *courtoisie* that take Yeats back to the Elizabethans and the Italian and French Renaissance he loved so well.

Finally, what can one do, more than to praise and to point, when a single poet can turn out pure lyrics so perfect yet so different in character as "To a Young Beauty," "The Dawn," "A Deep-sworn Vow," "The Mother of God," and "Remorse for Intemperate Speech"? What other poet would wish, or would dare to wish, that he might dine at journey's end with *both* Landor and John Donne? [16]

To sense the variety within these rude categories, take "A Prayer for My Daughter" from the leisurely meditative poems, "Byzantium" from among the longer and "Leda and the Swan" from among the shorter symbolic poems, "A Dialogue of Self and Soul" to illustrate the debates, "Meditations in Time of Civil War" for the poem in separate movements. Where else in English lyric poetry is such range to be found?

In his later work, Yeats refines beyond refinement. Impurities had been burned away in the poems of his great quarter-century. Now some of the solid ore is burned away too. The pure singing verse carries quintessential passion. The "fine delight" no longer "fathers thought," or perhaps more accurately, thought is melted in this incandescence, "live and lancing like the blowpipe flame." Yeats's deepest artistic instinct, his lyricism, is left unadulterated at last, and there remains, still to use Hopkins' words, "the roll, the rise, the carol, the creation." *Words for Music Perhaps* and *A Woman Young and Old* are struck off in the quintessence of his style; most of what is common to all poetry is dissolved away, and we are left with the bold sketched outline of the poet Yeats.

These poems may be read as simple lyrics. But to one familiar with what has gone before, they suggest far more than they state. The refrains and the stanzas have a wild gaiety and force; the actors move with a strange galvanic certainty, as if they were puppets manipulated by symbolic powers; pages of argument or months of meditation seem compressed into a single word; everything is a gay and savage condensation of song. Art is at play.

The phenomenon is not unique. Great artists have solid convictions that do not falter. "I do not think men change much in their deepest thought." Yet art is creation, not repetition. Each replaying of a central theme must add something new, must progress. In consequence, if a great artist lives long enough in his art, where a cycle of Cathay may be crowded into a few full and intense years on the calendar, he may reach a stage where art becomes too easy, or more accurately, where technique becomes a matter of course. If he is a lesser artist, he may start to copy himself, like Utrillo or Browning. But the greatest artists (and, if one considers the mental energy expended in their artistic careers, the oldest)—men like Shakespeare, Beethoven, Wagner—will finally turn to sketching at times. They will experiment with shortcuts. They will not develop fully again what they had previously brought as near perfection as their powers allowed. It is as if variants on their central ideas were no longer of prime importance or interest to them, but their art—the mere putting into action again of a technique in a mastered medium—remained an inexhaustible joy. May not this account for the unearthly music of the last periods, strange to us because we so rarely approach (if the phrase has any meaning at all) "pure art," in which form, technique, manner, almost outweigh content? Yeats in his last manner arouses some such speculation.

But again he defies final statement. In *Last Poems and Plays* (1940), though the dominant mood is a lyrical intransigence, there are spacious poems in the grand manner: "The Gyres," "Lapis Lazuli," "The Statues," "A Bronze Head," "The Circus Animals' Desertion," "Under Ben Bulben." The vital energy that he so much admired seemed to increase with the years. Or to put it in his own images, the great dance of the phases of the moon continued, the diametrically opposed hands on the great clockface went round, and as he himself, his Will, became older, his art, the antithetical Mask, became younger; as his Creative Mind suffered trials and grew ever surer, his Body of Fate yielded to his gay mastery. He becomes "a man you have never known—a man of genius, more gay, more miserable."

His collected poems are so rounded and ardent and brimming that in spite of the seeming smallness of the lyric form, they seek their parallels in the Medici chapel or the Beethoven quartettes more readily than in, say, the jewelled and metal art of Cellini. What qualities led to such accomplishment? Passionate thought, consistent technique, controlled concentration, deliberate delight in the exercise of art. These qualities the first four chapters have considered. Governing them all is a fifth trait—the lyrical bent—which Yeats did not so much cultivate as inherit. In the cradle, Apollo touched his mouth with honey. Few artists owe so much in equal amounts to both luck and skill, or again in Yeats's terms, to chance and choice. Yeats trained his extensive natural gifts with a cool and continued ferociousness. Somewhere Ruskin speaks of Giotto's campanile at Florence as that rare combination of grace and power; and though we have again turned to the other arts for illustration, such a balance of grace and power is what Yeats's lyrics also achieve.

In his search for beliefs, Yeats began with the attitude of uncertainty which is the needful blessing and curse of the artist. Keats has called it for Shakespeare "negative capability"—the capacity to live without despair or creedal commitment in the ambiguities, the mysteries, the dusty answers and inconsistencies of our mortal lot. This is the open mind of the lover, who is not subjugating and debasing the loved world to his own limiting desires; the open mind of the artist, who wishes to reflect and to represent, rather than to impose, and whose refraining from compulsion is rewarded by the power to make his "mirror-resembling dream." This is the open mind of the curious inquirer, the man imaginatively humble and receptive before the diversity of life, who can say as Yeats says: "I began occasionally telling people that one should believe whatever had been believed in all countries and periods, and only reject any part of it after much evidence, instead of starting all over afresh and only believing what one could prove." [17] * This awareness of alternatives and inexhaustible possibilities gives man his freedom. Man by nature continually creates ideal hypotheses, and will continue to do so even though some of his hypotheses reduce him to an animal or an automaton, a mouth or a hand. But the poet preserves the permanent human pattern; he will not permit man's perpetual hopes and aspirations to be reduced to any single grim narrow hypothesis labelled truth.

The acceptance of life in all its variety may be bewildering, and for a long time the young poet trod the road of the chameleon. But the choices became clearer, the tentative speculations fell gradually into patterns, and Yeats emerged with a confidence in himself, or in his creative imagination, which may best be called his courage. He emerged with beliefs (because he found that they squared with his experience) in aristocracy, desire, individuality, custom and ceremony, wholeness through oppositions, and immortality. To sum them up in a sentence, "We begin to live when we have conceived life as tragedy"— and tragedy is the simultaneous acceptance of man's limitations and man's infinite capacities. This, then, is "the image of our state."

How shall such a faith be cast into the forms of art? Through symbols. The symbol for Yeats is so inclusive in its powers and purposes that he regards it with almost mystical veneration. In theory it presents indistinguishably the sharp particularity of experience and the sense of permanent spiritual significance. The fine line of the chiseller suggests the boundless. The inexhaustible past and future are caught in a moment's image. And these symbols, springing unbidden to the mind, slowly growing, forming their own antitheses, crystallizing with other symbols into dominating single patterns, ineffable, moral, through the very paradox of their implausibility magically evoke revelations of reality.

Surely this is a terrific burden to lay upon what, narrowly considered, is a common device for verbal communication— the metaphor! Only in practice may such a theory be justified; Yeats's practice justifies the theory. Any of his symbols may be traced in its slow growth, its ramifications above ground and its exploring roots below, its increasing articulation. The antitheses and antinomies may even build themselves together, so that two rose-trees may so merge that they seem sprung from but a single root— or even three bushes may intermingle until no one who plucks one of their roses may know where its roots began.[18] "How can we know the dancer from the dance?" Is the great rooted chestnut tree "the leaf, the blossom or the bole?" [19] In the great complex emblems of the tree, the dance, the mummy, the flame, the fountain, Yeats triumphs in the instantaneous awareness of the transient and the eternal. The steady development of both thought and symbols, their consistency and coherence through a variety of individual poems, the deliberate technique of making all of his lyrics parts of one family (as he conceives his own thought to be but a part, a reflection, of the human inheritance) allow Yeats to shape the delicate lyric into a form not unworthy of comparison to epic and tragedy in their more majestic proportions

Everywhere the demand for compression, for marmorean stillness, for lyrical stasis, for the unity of a cut agate. Only through the device of repetition and echoing could Yeats pour such intense passion and such brooding thought into so small a vessel. The appreciation of his lyrics demands a criticism acknowledging that some forms of poetry are not essentially dramatic, that some poems cannot be considered as pastiches, that irony is not the sole secret of intensity or even of comprehensiveness, and that analytical methods and the assumption of complexity (in the sense that a magpie's nest is complex) may betray the lyrical drive toward intense simplicity and compressed form.

Finally, what is the purpose of art? Revelation. Revelation through joy. Joy through an act of creation, and an awareness of that act. Thus once more is man affirmed as a spirit. And thus he beholds an image of his state. Art again affirms life in its essence. The phantasmagoria dissolves; the unbearable transience of mortality is met by resolution. "Now more than ever seems it rich to die," but through art death has been transmuted into joy,[20] * and the tragic mystery has become a triumph. In the artist's "continual deliberate self-delighting happiness," to the end of the world "strength shall laugh and wisdom mourn." [21] In Yeats the creative act is not an act of withdrawal or of limitation, but of affirmation; sweetness must come with a knowledge of bitterness as well. The road of this poet leads from the songs of experience to the songs of radical innocence.

The world has been acknowledged: the best lack all conviction, while the worst are full of passionate intensity. Night closes round, and the swan drifts upon a darkening flood. Yet light forms in the word, cold and passionate as the dawn. A bird's sleepy cry is lost among the deepening shades, but the ear catches the exultant voice of a golden nightingale, singing of what is past or passing or to come.

NOTES

NOTES

The commonplaces of literary criticism, whether paraphrased or quoted directly, are not noted here. Neither are Yeats's well-known poems, or those quoted more than once or paraphrased. Whenever Yeats's development is in question, the dates of his separate poems are given in the text or the notes—the dates of the volumes in which they are first included, unless Yeats himself attaches a date to a poem. For consistency and clarity, the dates and "volumes" are those given in the *Collected Poems* and the *Last Poems* (Macmillan, 1933 and 1940). Wherever possible, quotations follow the *Collected Poems* because it is most easily accessible and because this study focuses on Yeats's coherent maturity. Yeats was in the habit of revising his early work, and was careless about dates. Those who wish more exact dates and earlier readings should consult William M. Roth's *A Catalogue of English and American First Editions of William Butler Yeats*, New Haven, 1939.

The footnotes starred in the text indicate that the note is more than a simple identification of source and that it includes additional illustrative material.

The principal editions of Yeats which have been used, together with their abbreviations, are given below. Unless specifically mentioned, these editions are used for page references.

Ideas of Good and Evil [*IGE*], 1903, 2d ed., A. H. Bullen, London.
The Cutting of an Agate [*C of A*], 1919, Macmillan, London.
Essays, 1924, Macmillan, New York. Includes: *Ideas of Good and Evil* [*IGE*] (1896–1903); *The Cutting of an Agate* [*C of A*] (1903–1915); *Per Amica Silentia Lunae* (1916–1917).
Autobiographies [*ABs*], 1927, Macmillan, New York. Includes: *Reveries over Childhood and Youth* [*Reveries*] (1914; Roth gives the first edition as 1915); *The Trembling of the Veil* [*T of V*] (1922).

The Collected Poems of W. B. Yeats [CP], 1933, Macmillan, New
   York.
The Collected Plays of W. B. Yeats, 1934, Macmillan, London.
A Vision, 1938, Macmillan, New York. (Begun in 1917, often re-
   vised, and dated 1936 at the end.)
Last Poems and Plays [LP], 1940, Macmillan, New York.

CHAPTER ONE

1. This book concentrates on Yeats as a man who achieved poetry,
since such deliberate efforts may be profitably studied; and concentrates even more narrowly on the mature and certain Yeats looking
back over his earlier career. It is harder to say anything about the
"born poet" that makes critical sense. To consider the occasions
that thrust poetry upon Yeats, the focus should be upon the relation
of his art to his life and his times, as in the excellent critical study
by Richard Ellmann, *Yeats: The Man and the Masks*, 1948, Macmillan, New York. Mr. Ellmann's book is invaluable for its inclusion of
unpublished or inaccessible material by Yeats, and for its clear
presentation of the interplay between Yeats's life and works.

2. Quoted from Mary Colum, *Life and the Dream*, Doubleday, 1947.

3. Since writing the above, I have read an article by Raphael Demos
which makes many of the points of this essay in terms much more
acceptable philosophically: "The Spectrum of Knowledge," in the
Philosophical Review, vol. LVI, no. 3, May 1947, pp.237–59. Of
Plato Mr. Demos says: "The Platonic dialogue is painted in all the
colors of the spectrum of thought." I would not agree with Mr.
Demos in his terms, which set up poesy as the purely concrete pole
against the abstractions of science, with Bacon's "philosophy" in a
mediate position. But he modifies his schematization in phrases with
which I would whole-heartedly concur: that although "poesy is the
only mode [of cognition] which apprehends the individual," yet
"I am making the double statement that poesy is cognitive, and
that it is cognitive of the individual."

4. Yeats is keenly aware both of fashions of thought and of individual bents. "But now that *The Golden Bough* has made Christianity look modern and fragmentary we study Confucius with Ezra
Pound, or like T. S. Eliot find in Christianity a convenient sym-

bolism for some older or newer thought, or say with Henry Air-bubble 'I am a member of the Church of England but not a Christian.' " *The Ten Principal Upanishads*, put into English by Shree Purohit Swami and Yeats, 1937, Macmillan, p.10.

5. Yeats realizes the strenuous process of creation. "It has only been of late years [he is writing about 1922] that I have found it possible to face an hour's verse without a preliminary struggle and much putting off." *ABs*, p.464. From "The Stirring of the Bones" in *T of V*: Much of this pain in creation comes from the energy exhausted in choosing among hypotheses. Just as Wordsworth (so his sister Dorothy wrote) made himself ill searching for the right words to describe the song of the cuckoo, so Yeats tells us that when he first went to Lady Gregory's to recuperate, he had outrun his strength, not in the arts and in thought only, but in actual physical health. "It is not so much that I choose too many elements, as that the possible unities themselves seem without number." p.463.

6. 1924, from the 6th edition.

7. For an extreme statement of this position, see Yeats's own creed as a young man, formulated between 1887 and 1891: "I had even created a dogma: 'Because those imaginary people are created out of the deepest instinct of man, to be his measure and his norm, whatever I can imagine those mouths speaking may be the nearest I can go to truth.' " *ABs*, p.143. From *T of V*, 1922.

8. Compare Yeats's own phrase on the maturing of thought: ". . . certain thoughts so long habitual that I may be permitted to call them my convictions." *Per Amica Silentia Lunae*, 1917, Prologue. The published letters of John Butler Yeats to his son (Faber and Faber, 1944) are well worth reading to see the development of Yeats's thought. The published letters to Dorothy Wellesley (Oxford University Press, 1940) are even more interesting for the light they shed on the genesis and growth of his later poems, as well as of the thought and purposes behind them. Richard Ellmann cogently compresses the influence of John Butler Yeats upon his son. In his book *Yeats: The Man and the Masks* (Macmillan, 1948, pp. 207–08), Mr. Ellmann writes of Yeats: "He began to see at last that his father's exaltation of personality, his use of psychological terms, his belief in a totality of being in which intellect was only a part, and his insistence that the poet should be free of his beliefs,

implied that poetry was an alogical method of discourse; and he instinctively understood that his father's theories had made his own symbolical method not only a possibility but a necessity."

9. "I exalted Mask and Image above the eighteenth-century logic, . . . and set experience before observation, emotion before fact." *ABs*, p.262. From *T of V*.

10. *Life and the Dream*, Doubleday, 1947, p.127.

11. "Active virtue, as distinguished from the passive acceptance of a code, is therefore theatrical, consciously dramatic, the wearing of a mask." *Essays*, p.497. In this passage from *Per Amica Silentia Lunae*, 1916–1917, Yeats says he is quoting his own words found "in an old diary." Evidently his theory of the Mask is a life-long conviction.

12. To understand more fully the place of freedom in what often looks like a deterministic system, see the references to the Thirteenth Cone, Sphere, or Cycle scattered through *A Vision*, but particularly on p.210, where Yeats feels the need for "deliverance," and on p.302, where Yeats says that the thirteenth sphere "is in every man and called by every man his freedom."

13. *A Full Moon in March*, 1935, p.26.

14. Though in a footnote I shall, and hereby do, record that in developing his philosophical theory of history and its presuppositions, Yeats refers to such men as Hegel, Scott (the editor of the Hermetic Fragments), Collyns Simon, Bishop Berkeley, Grosseteste, Pierre Duhem, Plotinus, Balzac, Flinders Petrie, Frobenius, Hermann Schneider, Toynbee, Croce, Marx, Heraclitus, Giovanni Gentile, Kant, Spengler, Wyndham Lewis, Vico, Leibnitz, Taylor (the editor of Plato), F. H. Bradley, Porphyry, Anaximander, Empedocles, Nicholas of Cusa, Plato, Hipparchus, Ptolemy, Plutarch, Josef Strzygowski, Dante, Gerald Heard, Sorel, and Henry Adams.

15. *A Vision*, p.296.   18. *Ibid.*, p.205.

16. *Ibid.*, p.296.   19. *Ibid.*, pp.212–13.

17. *Ibid.*, p.221.

20. *Ibid.*, p.205. The status of his belief in *A Vision* is also apparent in what he says outside the book itself, as when he refers to "my

Lunar parable" or says "for a constant return to our life is part of my dream," still speaking of *A Vision.—ABs*, p.425. From *T of V*, 1922.

21. *Ibid.*, p.19.   24. *Ibid.*, p.13.

22. *Ibid.*, p.8.   25. *Ibid.*, pp. 17–18.

23. *Ibid.*, p.10.   26. *Ibid.*, p.19.

27. "They once told me not to speak of any part of the system, except of the incarnations which were almost fully expounded, because if I did the people I talked to would talk to other people, and the communicators would mistake that misunderstanding for their own thought." pp.11–12.

28. *Ibid.*, p.20.

29. For those who find *A Vision* unnecessarily difficult going, and for those who are interested in the genesis of poetic convictions, *Per Amica Silentia Lunae* (1916–17) is richly rewarding. The ideas of the Mask, of antitheses, and of desire, come out strongly. Anyone can understand his ideas and illustrations when he says of Lady Gregory: "To me it seems that her ideal of beauty is the compensating dream of a nature wearied out by over-much judgement." Or: "William Morris, a happy, busy, most irascible man, described dim colour and pensive emotion, following, beyond any man of his time, an indolent muse; while Savage Landor topped us all in calm nobility when the pen was in his hand, as in the daily violence of his passion when he had laid it down." No wonder that here also we find his famous statement: "We make out of the quarrel with others, rhetoric, but of the quarrel with ourselves, poetry."—*Essays*, pp.487, 489, 492.

30. *Ibid.*, p.22.

31. The old Arab who takes Robartes into his tribe "belonged to a tribe of Arabs who called themselves Judwalis or Diagrammatists because their children are taught dances which leave upon the sand traces full of symbolical meaning." p.41.

32. *Ibid.*, p.33.   34. *Ibid.*, p.48.

33. *Ibid.*, p.42.

35. *Ibid.*, p.23. Compare also: "Natural and supernatural with the self-same ring are wed." "Supernatural Songs," No. 2, in *A Full Moon in March*, 1935, p.63.

36. *Ibid.*, p.301, which is also paraphrased or quoted in the rest of this paragraph and the succeeding one.

37. "The passions, when we know that they cannot find fulfilment, become vision; and a vision, whether we wake or sleep, prolongs its power by rhythm and pattern."—*Essays*, p.505. From *Per Amica Silentia Lunae*.

38. These generalizations, and the argument of this book, consider Yeats in his full achievement from almost the age of fifty on. The judgments would be modified considerably by those who set a higher value on his early work than the mature Yeats himself set.

39. Yeats, who felt that his Daimon (which in one sense was his art) drew him, as do all our Daimons, "to whatever among works not impossible is the most difficult," believed that neither faith nor beauty were easily achieved: "We must not make a false faith by hiding from our thoughts the causes of doubt, for faith is the highest achievement of the human intellect, the only gift man can make to God, and therefore it must be offered in sincerity. Neither must we create, by hiding ugliness, a false beauty as our offering to the world. He only can create the greatest imaginable beauty who has endured all imaginable pangs."—*Essays*, pp.529 and 494. From *Per Amica Silentia Lunae*. The last sentence quoted blends his idea of aristocracy with the idea of the strenuous bravery of the artist.

40. That Yeats's haughty aristocrat is such because of the possession of hard-won spiritual qualities, particularly of courage, may be seen in such passing remarks as: "The movement of letters had been haughty even before Magic had touched it. Rimbaud had sung: 'Am I an old maid that I should fear the embrace of death?' "—*Essays*, p.537. From the Epilogue to *Per Amica Silentia Lunae*. And, speaking of the conquest of the Norman aristocrats by the English bourgeois Puritan spirit: "Now it was to overthrow their beautiful haughty imagination and their manners, full of abandon and wilfulness, and to set in their stead earnestness and logic and the timidity and reserve of a counting-house."—*C of A*, p.227, 1912 ed. From "Edmund Spenser," 1902. Yeats's attitude toward the common Irish

people is perhaps best suggested in the essay "Poetry and Tradition" (1907), included in *The Cutting of an Agate*.

41. "The poet finds and makes his mask in disappointment, the hero in defeat. The desire that is satisfied is not a great desire, nor has the shoulder used all its might that an unbreakable gate has never strained."—*Essays*, p.500. From *Per Amica Silentia Lunae*.

42. This recurring symbol is explained in greatest detail, involving the whole pull between sun and moon, and the idea of effort as well as desire, in "The Stirring of the Bones" (in *T of V*; *ABs*, pp.456 ff.).

43. That Yeats does not consider individuality incompatible with the cosmic pattern comes out in his sentence: "The next morning I awoke near dawn, to hear a voice saying, 'The love of God is infinite for every human soul because every human soul is unique, no other can satisfy the same need in God.' "—*ABs*, p.465. From "The Stirring of the Bones," in *T of V*, 1922. The strain between discovering truth in the individual and turning it into impersonal art comes out in two such opposed sentences as these:
"I . . . believe that poetry and romance cannot be made by the most conscientious study of famous moments and the thoughts and feelings of others, but only by looking into that little, infinite, faltering, eternal flame that we call ourselves."
" . . . and yet a man is a great man just in so far as he can make his mind reflect everything with indifferent precision like a mirror."
—*Stories of Red Hanrahan*, pp.78 and 205 in 1914 ed. From his dedication to AE, 1896 ed., and his "Rosa Alchemica."

44. Essay on "Magic," *IGE*, 1903 ed., p. 29.

45. Compare: "Elaborate modern psychology sounds egotistical, I thought, when it speaks in the first person, but not those simple emotions which resemble the more, the more powerful they are, everybody's emotion, and I was soon to write many poems where an always personal emotion was woven into a general pattern of myth and symbol."—*ABs*, p.187. From *T of V*, 1922.
Yeats's sense of humor and his mature sense of fact also saved him from egotism: "I had a black fortnight . . . & spent my day in bed & thought of my soul. Then I noticed that every time I thought of my soul I used some second-hand phrase & knew by

that that I was thinking of my soul from ambition & vanity. I said to myself 'Your job is to avoid deep places & to die blaspheming' & I got well at once."—*Letters to Dorothy Wellesley*, p.124.

46. Yeats thinks of himself as even more traditional than the traditionalists. "Have not my thoughts," he asks in 1917, "run through a like round [the affirmation of nationalism and religion, Mother France and Mother Church], thought I have not found my tradition in the Catholic Church, which was not the church of my childhood, but where the tradition is, as I believe, more universal and more ancient?"—*Essays*, p. 538. From *Per Amica Silentia Lunae*. See also "Poetry and Tradition" (1907) in *The Cutting of an Agate*, in which he identifies the artist with tradition (Section II).

47. As early as 1916–17, Yeats is fully aware of the need for wholeness-through-oppositions in the distinction he makes between the realist and "any great poetical writer." "A realist," he says, "is an historian and obscures the cleavage by the record of his eyes."—*Essays*, p. 489. From *Per Amica Silentia Lunae*.

48. "The Daemon comes not as like to like but seeking its own opposite, for man and Daemon feed the hunger in one another's hearts. Because the ghost is simple, the man heterogeneous and confused, they are but knit together when the man has found a mask whose lineaments permit the expression of all the man most lacks, and it may be dreads, and of that only."—*Essays*, p.498. From *Per Amica Silentia Lunae*, which should be read entire to trace the importance of this idea in Yeats's thought.

49. The slow and unwilled shaping of his convictions is evident throughout his work. For example: "It was at Coole that the first few simple thoughts that now, grown complex through their contact with other thoughts, explain the world, came to me from beyond my own mind."—*ABs*, p.464. From "The Stirring of the Bones" in *T of V*, 1922.

50. This note is designed for those who watch straws to see how the wind blows, and who feel that *le petit fait significatif* may often make clear some large general truth. The large question here is possibility, potentiality, as a necessary part of reality humanly apprehended. The artist, as a poser of "Perhaps," is a realist. It is interesting to note how frequently the little word

"maybe" (or the variant "it may be") occurs in Yeats's lyrics. I have noted it, in the 1933 *Collected Poems*, on pp.180, 194, 195, 202, 203, 204, 210, 216, 232, 242, 266. The list is not exhaustive. In three cases (202, 232, 266) the accent seems to fall on the first syllable: *may*be. In three cases (195, 216, 242) on the last: may*be*. In the other five cases, the accent seems to hover, and in four of them the word is deliberately used twice, once with each possibility. In a poem, "Solomon and the Witch," which contains the lines:

> May*be* an image is too strong
> Or *may*be is not strong enough,

he is a bold metrist who will determine whether the initial foot in an earlier line: "Maybe the bride-bed brings despair" is an iamb or a trochee. The spondaic reading would seem safest. Perhaps readers will agree that "Or maybe substance can be composite," even in metrics. It may be that Yeats's gradual crystallization towards certainty is indicated by such a trivial phenomenon as his use of the word in *Last Poems and Plays* (1940). In four instances here (pp.8, 9, 67, 82) it seems definitely: *may*be. In only one instance (p.80) does there seem a question. It may be that the hovering accent in so many poems indicates through minute details of technique the whole hovering poetic world of "perhaps." But again, maybe not.

51. "Nor has any poet I have read of or heard of or met with been a sentimentalist. The other self, the anti-self or the antithetical self, as one may choose to name it, comes but to those who are no longer deceived, whose passion is reality. . . . For the awakening, for the vision, for the revelation of reality, tradition offers us a different word—ecstasy."—*Essays*, p.493. From *Per Amica Silentia Lunae*, 1916–17.

CHAPTER TWO

1. "All symbolic art should arise out of a real belief, and that it cannot do so in this age proves that this age is a road and not a resting-place for the imaginative arts." *C of A*, p.106. From "Discoveries," 1906.

2. *IGE*, p.176. From "William Blake and His Illustrations to *The Divine Comedy*." On the qualitative distinction that Yeats often draws between allegory and symbolism, he writes: "I find that though I love symbolism, which is often the only fitting speech for some mystery of disembodied life, I am for the most part bored by allegory, which is made, as Blake says, 'by the daughters of memory,' and coldly, with no wizard frenzy."—*C of A*, p.253, 1912 ed. From "Edmund Spenser," 1902. Compare also: "Allegory and, to a much greater degree, symbolism are a natural language by which the soul when entranced, or even in ordinary sleep, communes with God and with angels. They can speak of things which cannot be spoken of in any other language, but one will always, I think, feel some sense of unreality when they are used to describe things which can be described as well in ordinary words."—*Ibid*., pp.231–32.

Since Yeats makes neither a practicable mechanical separation nor a functional distinction between allegory and symbolism, one may assume that ordinarily he uses the two terms to make qualitative judgments: allegory is partially successful symbolism.

3. *Wheels and Butterflies*, p.103, pref. to *The Resurrection*. Yeats's note on this sentence reads: "Afterwards described in my poem 'The Second Coming'."

4. *IGE*, p.29. From the essay on "Magic." The Great Mind and the Great Memory, Yeats believes, may be evoked by symbols. Compare also: ". . . that great memory, which is still the mother of the Muses, though men no longer believe in it."—*Ibid*., p.133. From "The Philosophy of Shelley's Poetry," 1900.

5. *IGE*, pp.90–91. From "The Philosophy of Shelley's Poetry," 1900.

6. *IGE*, p.196. From "William Blake and His Illustrations," 1897. Compare also: "an emotion does not exist, or does not become perceptible and active among us, till it has found its expression." *Ibid*., p.244. From "The Symbolism of Poetry," 1900. To show the persistence of this notion of indivisibility, compare Yeats's statement 37 years later, now linking belief and expression: "Yet I am satisfied; I have escaped that polyglot, hyphenated, latinised, muddied muddle of distortion [bad translations] that froze belief. Can we believe or disbelieve until we have put our thought into a language wherein we are accustomed to express love and hate and

all the shades between?"—*The Ten Principal Upanishads*, put into English by Shree Purohit Swami and Yeats, Macmillan, 1937, Preface, p.8.

7. *C of A*, p.22. From "Certain Noble Plays of Japan," April, 1916. Compare also: "All Art that is not mere story-telling, or mere portraiture, is symbolic, . . . for it entangles, in complex colours and forms, a part of the Divine Essence."—*IGE*, p.230. From "Symbolism in Painting," 1898. In modern literature, Yeats says in 1906, "we have lost in personality, in our delight in the whole man—blood, imagination, intellect, running together."—*C of A*, p.66. From "Discoveries."

8. *C of A*, p.94. From "Discoveries," 1906.

9. *Ibid.*, p.104. From "The Thinking of the Body" in "Discoveries."

10. Regarding the unity of the race, since Chaucer's day, Yeats believes that the common European mind and heart has been fractured by "abstraction," by which he partially means "the isolation of occupation, or class or faculty." Yet even today or in the future, "a nation or an individual with great emotional intensity might . . . give to all those separated elements and to all that abstract love and melancholy, a symbolical, a mythological coherence." "To-day I add to that first conviction, to that first desire for unity, this other conviction, long a mere opinion vaguely or intermittently apprehended: Nations, races, and individual men are unified by an image, or bundle of related images, symbolical or evocative of the state of mind, which is of all states of mind not impossible, the most difficult to that man, race, or nation; because only the greatest obstacle that can be contemplated without despair, rouses the will to full intensity." *ABs*, pp.236, 239, 241. From *T of V*, 1922. This is a poet's statement of Toynbee's theory of challenge and response.

Regarding the unity of the artist or individual, Yeats holds that poet and philosopher share "the necessity of speaking the whole mind or remaining silent or ineffective." "I still think that in a species of man, wherein I include myself, nothing so much matters as Unity of Being."—*Ibid.*, pp.439, 435. From "The Stirring of the Bones," in *T of V*.

11. *IGE*, p.239. From "The Symbolism of Poetry," 1900.

12. Compare also: "All writers, all artists of any kind, in so far as they have had any philosophical or critical power, perhaps just in so far as they have been deliberate artists at all, have had some philosophy, some criticism of their art; and it has often been this philosophy, or this criticism, that has evoked their most startling inspiration." Or more sweepingly: "almost certainly no great art . . . has arisen without a great criticism."—*IGE*, pp.239–40. From "The Symbolism of Poetry," 1900.

On philosophy as supplying meaning in our relativistic transitional society, our "Road of the Chameleon," he writes: "He [Macgregor Mathers] had tried to prolong his youthful dream, had mounted into Hodos Chameliontos, and I have known none mount there and come to good that lacked philosophy."—*ABs*, p.417. From *T. of V.*

And on the relation between meaning and a serious subject matter: "I had been put into a rage by the followers of Huxley, Tyndall, Carolus Duran, and Bastien-Lepage, who . . . asserted the unimportance of subject whether in art or literature."—*ABs*, p.235. From *T of V.*

13. "Among School Children," 1928.

14. *IGE*, p.217. From "William Blake and His Illustrations," 1897.

15. "I have found in an old diary a saying from Stephane Mallarmé, that his epoch was troubled by the trembling of the veil of the Temple. As those words were still true, during the years of my life described in this book, I have chosen The Trembling of the Veil for its title."—*ABs*, p.135. From the Preface to *T of V*, dated May 1922. Compare his early story, *John Sherman*, in which the antagonist "could think carefully and cleverly, and even with originality, but never in such a way as to make his thoughts an allusion to something deeper than themselves. In this he was the reverse of poetical, for poetry is essentially a touch from behind a curtain." 1891, New York ed., p.100.

16. "He was at that marchland between waking and dreaming where our thoughts begin to have a life of their own—the region where art is nurtured and inspiration born."—*John Sherman*, 1891, New York ed., p.90.

Tragic art grafts upon the real world "images that remind us of vast passions, the vagueness of past times, all the chimeras that haunt the edge of trance."—*C of A*, p.33. From "The Tragic Theatre."

"Does not all art come when . . . something . . . suddenly starts into its place, something which is as unforeseen, as completely organised, even as unique, as the images that pass before the mind between sleeping and waking?"—*ABs*, p.410. From *T of V*, 1922.

"That which comes as complete, as minutely organised, as are those elaborate, brightly lighted buildings and sceneries appearing in a moment, as I lie between sleeping and waking, must come from above me and beyond me."—*Essays*, p.486. From *Per Amica Silentia Lunae*.

One might also compare Harry Levin's statement: "When Joyce first set out to write, he defined the double responsibility of the imaginative writer as a task of mediation between the world of reality and the world of dreams."—*James Joyce*, p.221, New Directions, 1941. This whole fine and final paragraph in Levin's book, pp.221–22, uses Yeats to define Joyce, and closes with an epitaph drawn from "The Tower."

17. "Yet it was a Yeats who spoke the only eulogy that turns my head: 'We have ideas and no passions, but by marriage with a Pollexfen we have given a tongue to the sea cliffs'."—*ABs*, p.27. From *Reveries*, 1914.

18. *C of A*, p.110. From "Discoveries," 1906, the section entitled "The Holy Places."

19. Joseph Hone's biography of Yeats, Macmillan, 1942, p.441.

20. *IGE*, pp.127–28. From "The Philosophy of Shelley's Poetry," 1900.

21. *IGE*, p.341. From "Emotion of Multitude," 1903.
Compare also: "poetry and imagination, always the children of far-off multitudinous things . . ." *Ibid.*, p.339.
". . . now writers have begun to dwell upon the element of evocation, of suggestion, upon what we call the symbolism in great writers."—*IGE*, p.241. From "The Symbolism of Poetry," 1900.

22. *C of A*, p.120. From "Preface to . . . [Synge's] The Well of the Saints," 1905.

23. *C of A*, pp.31–32. From "The Tragic Theatre," 1910.

24. "A poetical passage cannot be understood without a rich memory, and like the older school of painting appeals to a tradition, and that not merely when it speaks of 'Lethe's Wharf' or 'Dido on the wild sea-banks' but in rhythm, in vocabulary."— *C of A*, pp. 10–11. From "Certain Noble Plays of Japan," 1916.

25. *C of A*, p.35. From "The Tragic Theatre," 1910.

26. Yeats remembered with pleasure what Paul Verlaine said at Oxford: "Tennyson is too noble, too Anglais; when he should have been broken-hearted, he had many reminiscences."—*ABs*, p.423. From *T of V*, 1922.

   As a young man, Yeats felt his father had not gone far enough in mocking at Philistine morality; he should have destroyed it by serious argument: "One morning when my father was on the way to his studio, he met his landlord and they had this conversation: 'Do you think now that Tennyson should have been given that peerage?' 'One's only doubt is if he should have accepted it: it was a finer thing to be Alfred Tennyson.' There was a silence, and then: 'Well, all the people I know think he should not have got it.' Then, spitefully: 'What's the good of poetry?' 'Oh, it gives our minds a great deal of pleasure.' 'But wouldn't it have given your mind more pleasure if he had written an improving book?' 'Oh, in that case I should not have read it.' My father returned in the evening delighted with his story, but I could not understand how he could take such opinions lightly and not have seriously argued with the man."—*ABs*, pp.104–05. From *Reveries*, 1914.

   No narrow conception of morality appeals to Yeats, then, since he can write of Spenser that "He had been made a poet by what he had almost learnt to call his sins."—*C of A*, p.233, 1912 ed. From the essay on "Edmund Spenser," dated October, 1902. The bent of Yeats's own moral preferences is shown in this same essay when he contrasts the native English Puritan spirit with that of the Norman conquerors (quoted in part in Note 40 to Chapter One).

27. *IGE*, p.93. From "The Philosophy of Shelley's Poetry," 1900.
   Imagination as a moral instrument for evoking human sympathy is apparent elsewhere in Yeats: "If you liberate a person or a landscape from the bonds of motives and their actions, causes and

their effects, and from all bonds but the bonds of your love, it will change under your eyes, and become a symbol of an infinite emotion, a perfected emotion, a part of the Divine Essence."—*IGE*, p.231. From "Symbolism in Painting," 1898.

28. *IGE*, p.170. From "William Blake and the Imagination," 1897.

29. *IGE*, p.213. From "William Blake and His Illustrations," 1897.

30. "Count Tolstoy, in the books he wrote before he became a prophet and fell into a lesser order [than that of great writer]."—*IGE*, p.169. From "William Blake and the Imagination," 1897.

31. *IGE*, p.133. From "The Philosophy of Shelley's Poetry," 1900.

32. *IGE*, p.244. From "The Symbolism of Poetry," 1900.

33. *IGE*, pp.112–13. From "The Philosophy of Shelley's Poetry," 1900.

Compare also: "And this thought [that the lyric poet must take one of half a dozen traditional poses, the accumulated expression of the world] before it could be knowledge was an instinct."—*ABs*, p.108. From *Reveries*, 1914.

34. "I had as many ideas as I have now, only I did not know how to choose from among them those that belonged to my life."—*ABs*, p.103. From *Reveries*, 1914.

"But now image called up image in an endless procession, and I could not always choose among them with any confidence; and when I did choose, the image lost its intensity, or changed into some other image. . . . I was lost, . . . astray upon the Path of the Cameleon, upon *Hodos Chameliontos*."—*ABs*, pp. 334–35. From *T of V*, 1922.

35. One of Yeats's finest poems, "The Cat and the Moon," and perhaps his most distinguished piece of prose, *Per Amica Silentia Lunae* (1916–17), were crystallized by an incident that happened in the summer of 1916. I wonder if such crystallization may not have been helped by a finger-exercise more than a quarter of a century before: " 'Ah!' he thought, 'it would be a good thing to be a little black cat. To leap about in the moonlight and sleep in the sunlight, and catch flies, to have no hard tasks to do or hard decisions to come to, to be simple and full of animal spirits.' "—*John*

Sherman, p.55, 1891, New York ed. There, already, is the cat Minnaloushe in brief, except that Yeats has not learned to build tension through antinomies, and has pitched the story in a sodden mood, for "it deals with dull persons and the world's affairs."

Since this volume is hard to come by, it may be of interest to include here the prose version that shows the genesis of "The Lake Isle of Innisfree." The "he" is the titular hero of *John Sherman*:

"Delayed by a crush in the Strand, he heard a faint trickling of water near by; it came from a shop window where a little water-jet balanced a wooden ball upon its point. The sound suggested a cataract with a long Gaelic name, that leaped crying into the Gate of the Winds at Ballah. . . . It [an osier-covered Chiswick islet on the Thames] made him remember an old daydream of his. The source of the river that passed his garden at home was a certain wood-bordered and islanded lake, whither in childhood he was often gone blackberry-gathering. At the further end was a little islet called Inniscrewin. Its rocky center, covered with many bushes, rose some forty feet above the lake. Often when life and its difficulties had seemed to him like the lessons of some elder boy given to a younger by mistake, it had seemed good to dream of going away to that islet and building a wooden hut there and burning a few years out, rowing to and fro, fishing, or lying on the island slopes by day, and listening at night to the ripple of the water and the quivering of the bushes—full always of unknown creatures—and going out at morning to see the island's edge marked by the feet of birds."—pp.105–07.

36. *IGE*, p.126. From "The Philosophy of Shelley's Poetry," 1900.

37. *Ibid.*, p.98.

38. *Ibid.*, pp.140–41. Compare also: "I have often had the fancy that there is some one Myth for every man, which, if we but knew it, would make us understand all he did and thought. Shakespeare's Myth, it may be, describes a wise man who was blind from very wisdom, and an empty man who thrust him from his place, and saw all that could be seen from every emptiness."—*IGE*, p.162. From "At Stratford-on-Avon," 1901. This subtle observation Yeats illustrates by setting up Hamlet and Richard II against Fortinbras and Henry V. It seems equally applicable in *Othello*, *Lear*, and *Antony and Cleopatra*.

39. This idea is most fully developed in Yeats's long essay, "The Philosophy of Shelley's Poetry," 1900, which is considered at greater length in the next chapter. In sum: "There is hardly indeed a poem of any length in which one does not find it [Shelley's symbol of Morning and Evening Star] as a symbol of love, or liberty, or wisdom, or beauty, or of some other expression of that Intellectual Beauty, which was to Shelley's mind the central power of the world."—*IGE*, p.130. Realization of the persistence and power of this symbol, for example, would have kept T. S. Eliot from his complete misunderstanding and damning of Shelley's stanza in the Skylark ode: "Like the silver arrows . . ."

40. *The Oxford Book of Modern Verse*, Oxford University Press, 1936, pp. xix *et seq.*, Introduction.

41. *IGE*, p.242. From "The Symbolism of Poetry," 1900.

42. *IGE*, pp.306–07. From "The Moods," 1895.
Compare also: "Art is a revelation, and not a criticism."—*IGE*, p.310 From "The Body of the Father Christian Rosencrux," 1895.
Yeats believes that the modern symbolist poet is "a foreshadower of the new sacred book, of which all the arts, as somebody has said, are begging to dream, and because, as I think, they cannot overcome the slow dying of men's hearts that we call the progress of the world, and lay their hands upon men's heart-strings again, without becoming the garment of religion as in old times."—*IGE*, p.253. From "The Symbolism of Poetry," 1900. On p.294 he thinks that the "somebody" he quotes is Verhaeren.

43. *ABs*, pp.336–37. From *T of V*, 1922.

44. A slight indication of Yeats's idiosyncratic manner of dealing with "the main track of thought and expression" may be found in Yeats's habit, Richard Ellmann tells us in *Yeats: The Man and the Masks* (Macmillan, 1948), of pronouncing "gyre" with a hard g. Throughout his life, his spelling was equally his own.

45. As an example of the clarity and organizing thought which his symbols introduce into his poetry, consider these lines from an early poem, "The Two Trees," as it is printed in *Collected Poems* under the heading and date of *The Rose*, 1893:

> There the Loves a circle go,
> The flaming circle of our days,
> Gyring, spiring to and fro
> In those great ignorant leafy ways.

This revision has grown out of such earlier uncertainties as:

> There, through bewildered branches go,
> Winged Loves borne on in gentle strife,
> Tossing and tossing to and fro
> The flaming circle of our life.
> —*Poems*, Boston, 1895.

46. If anyone has the often reprinted 1933 volume of *Collected Poems*, Macmillan, New York, at hand, the following page references, though not exhaustive, might help to show how such grouped symbols grow, recur, and become clear and dominant. Gyre: 55, (82), 213, 214, 215, 223, 273. Circles: 234, 240, (256), 276. Whirl: 265, 280, 313. Wind, unwind, spindle: 165, 240, 243, 263, 266, 273, 302. Pern: 165, 213, 214, 223. Bobbin: 285. Spool: 254. Skein: 296. Spinning-jenny: 247. Spinning top: 196, (306).

47. Note to "The Dolls," *Responsibilities*, 1914.

48. This complicated tangle of symbols may be helped by a little prose: "Hafiz cried to his beloved, 'I made a bargain with that brown hair before the beginning of time, and it shall not be broken through unending time,' and it may be that Mistress Nature knows that we have lived many times, and that whatsoever changes and winds into itself belongs to us. She covers her eyes away from us, but she lets us play with the tresses of her hair." —*C of A*, pp. 100–01. From "Discoveries," 1906. This is the whole section called "The Tresses of the Hair." More than a quarter-century later, they still persist: "Berenice's burning hair" in "Her Dream," the eternal "bargain with that hair And all the windings there" in "His Bargain," Numbers XIII and XIV of *Words for Music Perhaps*, 1933.

49. "All Souls' Night," from *The Tower* (1928), also appears as the Epilogue to *A Vision*. For gyres leading to the idea of reincarnation or recurrence, see the use of "mummy" in section VIII of "Vacillation," *The Winding Stair*, 1933.

50. The diligent reader might look up in the *Collected Poems*: Blood: 192, 211, 214, 215, 218, 230, 236, 240, 244, 246, 273, 275, 285–86, 289, 308, 309, 314. Or for violent clustered ideas such as "frenzied seas" and "crazy meat": 128, 130, 197, 216, 217, 223, 243, (250), 283, 285–86.

51. The cavern imagery, which naturally associates with Yeats's stone imagery, takes on more meaning if one thinks also of Plato's cave, and of Yeats's own analysis of Shelley's repeated symbolic use of "cavern."—*IGE*, pp.90–141. "The Philosophy of Shelley's Poetry," 1900.

52. "Byzantium," 1933.

CHAPTER THREE

1. In *Ideas of Good and Evil*. The essay on Shelley is dated 1900. Subsequent quotations are from *IGE*, 1903 second edition, A. H. Bullen, London. The tesselation of quotations in succeeding paragraphs may be found, *seriatim*, on pp.123, 124, 127, 126, 125, 134-35, 140, 112-13, 98, 140-41, 128, 131, 119, 127-28, 111.

2. *CP*, p.444. Note to "He Mourns for the Change that has Come upon Him," in *The Wind Among the Reeds*, 1899.

3. *Letters on Poetry from W. B. Yeats to Dorothy Wellesley*, 1940, Oxford University Press, pp.94–95. The poem "To Dorothy Wellesley," may be found in *Last Poems*, 1940.

4. *C of A*, p.106. From "Discoveries," 1906, the section called "Religious Belief Necessary to Religious Art."

5. *C of A*, pp.19–21. From "Certain Noble Plays of Japan," 1916.

6. *C of A*, pp.28–29. From "The Tragic Theatre," 1910.

7. In *Last Poems and Plays*, 1940, p.112.

8. *Last Poems*, 1940, p.112.

9. *ABs*, pp.154–55. From *T of V*, 1922.

10. *ABs*, p.333. From *T of V*, 1922. This distilling of passion, this finding of quintessences, is suggested also in his statement con-

cerning "The Tragic Generation" of the 1890s: "I had put my
ideal of those years, an ideal that passed away with youth, into
my description of *Proud Costello*. 'He was of those ascetics of
passion, who keep their hearts pure for love or for hatred, as other
men for God, for Mary and for the Saints.' "—*ABs*, p.413. From
T of V, 1922. Though his asceticism also took other forms, to the
end of his life Yeats's strength depended upon his pure pride and
passion.

11. *C of A*, p.96. From "Discoveries," 1906.

12. *Ibid.*, p.110. For the idea of the impersonality of the artist,
compare also: "Does not all art come when a nature, that never
ceases to judge itself, exhausts personal emotion in action or desire
so completely that something impersonal, something that has nothing to do with action or desire, suddenly starts into its place . . .?"
—*ABs*, p.410. From *T of V*, 1922.

13. *C of A*, p.174. From "J. M. Synge and the Ireland of His
Time," 1910.

14. *Ibid.*, pp.145–46.

15. *ABs*, p.339. From *T of V*, 1922, "Hodos Chameliontos."

16. *ABs*, p.234. From *T of V*, 1922, "Four Years."

17. Not until this essay was shaped even to the extent of determin-
ing on this phrase did I read a passage in James Joyce which
illuminates what I am trying to say: "The instant wherein that
supreme quality of beauty, the clear radiance of the esthetic image,
is apprehended luminously by the mind which has been arrested
by its wholeness and fascinated by its harmony is the luminous
silent stasis of esthetic pleasure, . . . the enchantment of the heart."
—*A Portrait of the Artist as a Young Man*, p.250, Modern Library
edition.

Interesting also are Joyce's meditations, paralleling Yeats, regarding drama: "Pity is the feeling which arrests the mind in the
presence of whatsoever is grave and constant in human sufferings
and unites it with the human sufferer. Terror . . . unites it with
the secret cause. . . . You see I use the word *arrest*. I mean that
the tragic emotion is static. Or rather the dramatic emotion is.
The feelings excited by improper art are kinetic, desire or loath-

ing." In the aesthetic emotion of proper art, "The Mind is arrested and raised above desire and loathing." *Ibid.*, pp.239, 240. Aquinas's word *visa*, which covers aesthetic apprehensions of all kinds, "means certainly a stasis and not a kinesis. How about the true? It produces also a stasis of the mind." "These relations of the sensible, visible to you through one form and to me through another, must be therefore the necessary qualities of beauty."—*Ibid.*, pp.239, 240, 243, 245. I have since noticed that Harry Levin in his critical study of James Joyce (1941) also uses the headline term of "stasis" in explaining Joyce's art.

Joyce no less than Yeats does not distinguish between tragic emotions and successful theatre (unless we assume that Joyce felt successful theatre *invariably* was "improper art"). Unfortunately they do not coincide, though great drama contains both. These two Irishmen create strange new forms in the novel and the drama by bringing to those two *genres* their own lyrical gifts and their sense of pattern, rather than of narrative. As Gertrude Stein says: ". . . in the three novels written in this generation that are the important things written in this generation, there is, in none of them a story. There is none in Proust in The Making of Americans or in Ulysses."—Quoted by Thornton Wilder, p.xxv of his "Introduction" to Stein's *Four in America*, 1947.

18. "A Woman Young and Old," No. II, from *Collected Poems*, 1933. Compare also "Words for Music Perhaps," Nos. XIII and XIV, 1933.

19. "A Woman Young and Old," No. VI, in *CP*, 1933.

20. "The Man and the Echo," in *LP*, 1940.

21. "The Statues," in *LP*, 1940.

22. "Under Ben Bulben," in *LP*, 1940.

23. "The Statues," in *LP*, 1940.

24. *Ibid.* Compare: ". . . all ancient peoples, who like the old Irish had a nature more lyrical than dramatic. . . ."—*IGE*, p.285. From "The Celtic Element in Literature," 1902.

25. *IGE*, p.247. From "The Symbolism of Poetry," 1900.

26. Yeats's poems, even his plays, seem deliberately to avoid strict consciousness of time. This his theories would lead us to expect. Time, for Yeats as for Shakespeare, is the envious and calumniating robber who crams his rich thievery up; and thus may be felt as an antagonist. Positively, time is that medium within which an artist's convictions become clearer, his joy therefore greater, and his choices more his own. But since it intensifies the individual's awareness of his own accidental and consequently almost trivial state, poetry should try to disregard time or at most to blur its tyranny. In "The Wild Swans," for instance, careful reading is necessary to see that the second and third stanzas are laid primarily in the past, the final stanza in the future. How does Yeats know there are fifty-nine swans? On the evidence of the poem, I would say because he counted them nineteen years ago; but the second stanza is so cunningly wrought that it allows the reader almost to believe that the swans take flight "now," while Yeats looks at them. The third stanza is "now" and nineteen years ago. The fourth stanza is any time—it is the nature of the wild swans, still, unwearied still. And the last stanza is "now" and "some day" in the future. Since only the first stanza is laid in a single moment, and the rest are either double in time or disputable, Yeats has done his deliberate best to take the swans out of time without diminishing their precise and believable nature as 59 particular swans at Coole Park.

27. Two examples: The first time Yeats saw the swans, he "trod with a lighter tread." The illogical hidden sexual reference here to the treading of male swans may seem more legitimate if one remembers Yeats's "Leda and the Swan," or if one reads over again "Quarrel in Old Age" in which "that lonely thing," his beloved in her youth, "trod like Spring." Then one may turn to "His Phoenix" to learn of "that sprightly girl trodden by a bird."

"The still water" of the last stanza will suggest the Psalms without further help from Yeats; within the poem, the reader may catch the use here of "still" for "placid," and in the previous stanza for "yet," as Keats uses "still" with a double, perhaps a triple, ambiguity in "Thou still unravished bride of quietness." But the reader must go outside the poem to feel the full importance for Yeats in the fourth stanza of "still" to suggest continuing or permanent "passion or conquest," an example of his characteristic "lyrical stasis" or ecstasy.

28. To avoid bewildering bibliographical details, I use here, as elsewhere, the dates given in Yeats's *Collected Poems*. Actually, the Cuala Press edition of *The Wild Swans at Coole* was published October 10, 1917, and the Dun Emer edition of *In the Seven Woods*, which contains "The Withering of the Boughs," was published July 16, 1903.

29. A poet must be most punctilious to feel such an indebtedness should be acknowledged: "last reach" is the only verbal debt, plus the image of the long glittering river-track, for the idea of the dying swan is common property. More interesting, Sturge Moore's "brim, brim o'er" possibly governs "the brimming water" in the earlier "The Wild Swans at Coole."

30. "When You Are Old," in *The Rose*, 1893.

31. *W. B. Yeats*, Joseph Hone, 1942, Macmillan, p.425.

32. The reader might turn in *Collected Poems*, 1933, to pp.54, 89, 129, 140, 163–64, 179, 181, 185, 204, 230, 231, 234, 257, 261, 274, 312, 313, 316, for some references.

33. "Lapis Lazuli" and "The Pilgrim."

34. *Last Poems*, 1940. From "Under Ben Bulben," dated September 4, 1938.

CHAPTER FOUR

1. *C of A*, p.84. From "Discoveries," 1906.

2. *ABs*, p.107. From *Reveries*, 1914.

3. For its most extreme recent statement by a practicing poet, see W. H. Auden's essay "Squares and Oblongs" in *Poets at Work*, 1948, Harcourt, Brace; ed. Charles D. Abbott.

4. *Collected Plays*, p.127. From "The King's Threshold," 1904. Yeats says in the "Introductory Rhyme" to *Responsibilities*, 1914, that his grandfather Pollexfen's example taught him to say: "Only the wasteful virtues earn the sun."

5. *ABs*, pp.401–02. From "The Tragic Generation" in *T of V*, 1922. A beautiful summary of this and succeeding ideas comes in

"Poetry and Tradition," 1907. Aristocrats, country folk, and artists are the three types of men who have made all beautiful things. The rest of the people "fear irreverent joy and unserviceable sorrow. . . . They complain much of that commandment that we can do almost what we will, if we do it gaily. . . . That we may be free from all the rest, sullen anger, solemn virtue, calculating anxiety, gloomy suspicion, prevaricating hope, we should be reborn in gaiety. . . . We should sorrow alone over what is greater than ourselves, nor too soon admit that greatness, but all that is less than we are should stir us to some joy, for pure joy masters and impregnates; and so to world end, strength shall laugh and wisdom mourn."—*Essays*, pp.311-12. From *C of A*.

6. *C. of A*, p.250, 1912 ed. From "Edmund Spenser," 1902. Sheer vitality and the highest nobility are of course not mutually exclusive in Yeats's thought: "we artists, who are the servants not of any cause but of mere naked life, and above all of that life in its nobler forms, where joy and sorrow are one, Artificers of the Great Moment."—*Essays*, pp.321-22. From "Poetry and Tradition," 1907, in *C of A*.

7. *C of A*, pp.228-29, 1912 ed. From "Edmund Spenser," 1902.

8. *IGE*, p.162. From "At Stratford-on-Avon," 1901. This phrase comes from his interpretation of Shakespeare's attitude in creating the character of Henry V.

9. *ABs*, pp.174-75. From *T of V*, 1922. He admires Henley, as one would guess offhand, and largely because of this energy: "I see his crippled legs as though he were some Vulcan perpetually forging swords for other men to use."—*Ibid.*, p.158. And vitality as the shaping principle in an artist marks his adverse judgment on the historian York Powell: "He impressed all who met him, seemed to some a man of genius, but had not enough ambition to shape his thought, nor enough conviction to give rhythm to his style and remained always a poor writer."—*Ibid.*, p.145.

10. *C of A*, p.147. From "J. M. Synge and the Ireland of His Time," 1910.

11. *ABs*, p.425. From *T of V*, 1922.

12. *C of A*, p.142. From "J. M. Synge and the Ireland of His Time," 1910. The ideas of impersonal form and personal vitality also

blend in such an observation as this: "If one has not fine construction, one has not drama, but if one has not beautiful or powerful and individual speech, one has not literature, or, at any rate, one has not great literature. Rabelais, Villon, Shakespeare, William Blake, would have known one another by their speech. Some of them knew how to construct a story, but all of them had abundant, resonant, beautiful, laughing, living speech."—*C of A*, p.115. From "Preface to the Well of the Saints," 1905.

As a transition between art-as-action and art-as-deliberate-construction, consider these sentences of Jean-Paul Sartre, with which Yeats would probably have agreed: "To speak is to act: . . . words are 'loaded revolvers,' . . . If he speaks he fires. He can keep silent; but since he has chosen to fire, he has to aim properly and not close his eyes like a child who fires only for the joy of hearing the noise."—*Saturday Review of Literature*, Dec. 6, 1947. From "The Word as Mirror."

13. *C of A*, pp.v–vi. Dated December, 1918.

14. From *The Winding Stair*, 1933.

15. *C of A*, p.146. From "J. M. Synge and the Ireland of His Time," 1910.

16. *Oxford Book of Modern Verse*, 1936, p.xxxiv, Introduction.

17. *ABs*, p.392. From *T of V*, "The Tragic Generation." He is speaking of such friends as Dowson, Johnson, Horne, and Symons. Compare also, for his high conception of perfect lyrical craftsmanship, his impatience with Henley, who "never understood how small a fragment of our own nature can be brought to perfect expression, nor that even but with great toil, in a much divided civilization. . . . He would be, and have all poets be, a true epitome of the whole mass, . . . and because this . . . is no longer possible, his work lacks music, is abstract,"—*Ibid.*, p.364.

18. "I followed the career of a certain professional runner for months, buying papers that would tell me if he had won or lost. I had seen him described as 'the bright particular star of American athletics', and the wonderful phrase had thrown enchantment over him. Had he been called the particular bright star, I should have cared nothing for him."—*ABs*, p.48. From *Reveries*, 1914. (Yeats

knew, or learned, that "bright particular star" came from Shake-speare.)

19. Wordsworth's Preface to *Lyrical Ballads*.

20. *C of A*, p.72. From "Discoveries," 1906. He is quoting, so he says, from a lecture by Paul Verlaine at Oxford. Yeats further exalts his conception of style by arguing that freedom comes through mastery, and that style is a manifestation of ceremony, personal integrity, the control of the aristocrat (which is often popularly called "good form"): "In life courtesy and self-posses-sion, and in the arts style, are the sensible impressions of the free mind, for both arise out of a deliberate shaping of all things, and from never being swept away, whatever the emotion, into con-fusion or dullness. . . . A writer . . . should never be without style, which is but high breeding in words and in argument."—*C of A*, in *Essays*, 1924, p.313. From "Poetry and Tradition," 1907. And on p.314, the artist "has a continual deliberate self-delighting happiness—style, 'the only thing that is immortal in literature,' as Sainte-Beuve has said, a still unexpended energy, after all that the argument or the story needs, a still unbroken pleasure after the immediate end has been accomplished. . . ."

21. *C of A*, p.74. From "Discoveries," 1906. Compare: "You asked me about spiritual knowledge, I have explained it.

"Austerity, self-control, meditation are the foundation of this knowledge."

"Take the bow of our sacred knowledge, lay against it the arrow of devotion, pull the string of concentration, strike the target."—*The Ten Principal Upanishads*, pp.23 and 53, 1937. Put into English by Shree Purohit Swami and Yeats.

22. *C of A*, p.105. From "Discoveries," 1906, section entitled "Re-ligious Belief Necessary to Religious Art."

23. *C of A*, p.119. From the "Preface to the Well of the Saints," 1905.

24. *IGE*, p.90. From "The Philosophy of Shelley's Poetry," 1900.

25. *Poems*, 1912 ed., p.xi. From "Preface to the third edition," 1901.

26. *C of A*, p.74. From "Discoveries," 1906, the section entitled "The Tree of Life."

27. *Poems*, 1912 ed., pp. xi-xii. From "Preface to the third edition," 1901.

28. The quotations in this paragraph come from *C of A*, p.27. From "The Tragic Theatre," 1910; and from *Essays*, p.322. From "Poetry and Tradition," 1907.

Compare: "And I would have all know that when all falls
In ruin, poetry calls out in joy."
And:
"I need no help.
He needs no help that joy has lifted up
Like some miraculous beast out of Ezekiel.
The man that dies has the chief part in the story."

—*Collected Plays*, pp.114 and 141. From "The King's Threshold," 1904. More than thirty years later he writes: "In all the great tragedies, tragedy is a joy to the man who dies; in Greece the tragic chorus danced."—*Oxford Book of Modern Verse*, 1936, pp.xxxiv-v, Introduction.

29. This and succeeding quotations come from the group of poems in eight sections entitled "Vacillation," (1932) published in *The Winding Stair*, 1933.

30. This tree, "half all glittering flame and half all green Abounding foliage moistened with the dew," is one of Yeats's most powerful persistent images. Compare "The Two Trees" in *The Rose* (1893), or his description in *IGE*, pp.275-6, in which he reveals one source by quoting from the Mabinogion: "They saw a tall tree by the side of the river, one half of which was in flames from the root to the top, and the other half was green and in full leaf."

31. For his own prose parallel of this moment of ecstasy, compare: "At certain moments, always unforeseen, I become happy, most commonly when at hazard I have opened some book of verse. . . . Perhaps I am sitting in some crowded restaurant, the open book beside me, or closed, my excitement having over-brimmed the page. I look at the strangers near as if I had known them all my life, and it seems strange that I cannot speak to them: everything fills me with affection, I have no longer any fears or any needs; I do not even remember that this happy mood must come to an end."—*Essays*, p.533. From *Per Amica Silentia Lunae*, 1917, Section XXI.

32. Succeeding quotations are from this poem, which appeared in *The Wild Swans at Coole*, 1919.

33. This old theme of *Ubi sunt qui ante nos fuerunt?* Yeats frequently turns into a catalogue of courage. An example:

> Aye, and Achilles, Timor, Babar, Barhaim, all
> Who have lived in joy and laughed into the face of Death.
>> —"Upon a Dying Lady," VI: "Her Courage." *The Wild Swans at Coole*, 1919.

34. The last phrase is:

> but a thought
> Of that late death took all my heart for speech.

Does this mean: A thought took away all my desire to speak? Or: A thought took all my power in order to produce a poem? Or does it include both senses, the hopeless loss, and the resolve to set up a triumphant epitaph? In view of Yeats's sense of necessary conflict and necessary wholeness, a study of his purposeful ambiguities would be of value.

For instance, "Crazy Jane Talks with the Bishop" (*Words for Music Perhaps*, 1933) ends with the lines:

> For nothing can be sole or whole
> That has not been rent.

The first line, in the sense of the entire poem, might as well be written:

> For nothing can be soul or hole.

And for the ideas of transience and of wandering souls, an overtone on the word "rent" seems allowable—as in Eliot's sense in "Gerontion":

> Think at last
> We have not reached conclusion, when I
> Stiffen in a rented house.

35.   "And yet he had the *intensity*
>   To have published all to be a world's *delight*."
>   "And all he did *done perfectly*."

36. From "A Man Young and Old," Number X, *The Tower*, 1928. Other quotations in this paragraph are from "An Irish Airman," *The Wild Swans at Coole*, 1919. Compare also in that volume "Shepherd and Goatherd."

37. In *The Wild Swans at Coole*, 1919.

38. "Demon and Beast," in *Michael Robartes and the Dancer*, 1921.

39. "Tom O'Roughley," in *The Wild Swans at Coole*, 1919.

40. "Meditations in Time of Civil War," in *The Tower*, 1928.

41. "The Fisherman," in *The Wild Swans at Coole*, 1919.

42. "A Woman Young and Old," Number XI.

43. In *Michael Robartes and the Dancer*, 1921.

44. In *The Winding Stair*, 1933.

45. Compare also, for the relation of joy and age: "I have grown happier with every year of life as though gradually conquering something in myself, for certainly my miseries were not made by others but were a part of my own mind."—*ABs*, p.13. From *Reveries*, 1914.

Compare also "The Apparitions" in *Last Poems*, 1940:

> When a man grows old his joy
> Grows more deep day after day.

The artist has attained fullness and certainty. The question of death, however, opens its mystery and fright. Plato's ghost may still sing to the aging successful artist: "What then?" And the old man can but ask the cosmos, which merely echoes his thoughts:

> O Rocky Voice,
> Shall we in that great night rejoice?
> What do we know but that we face
> One another in this place?
> —"The Man and the Echo."

This theme of the mystery and fright is at least important enough for a note, for it occurs later than the more certain answer of "Sailing to Byzantium":

> Soul clap its hands and sing and louder sing
> For every tatter in its mortal dress.

But the brave positive answer of self-creation is still given, though now bitter, in "The Circus Animals' Desertion."

46. "That shaping joy has kept the sorrow pure, . . . for the nobleness of the Arts is in the mingling of contraries, the extremity of sorrow, the extremity of joy, perfection of personality, the perfection of its surrender, overflowing turbulent energy, and marmorean stillness; and its red rose opens at the meeting of the two beams of the cross, and at the trysting-place of mortal and immortal, time and eternity." Shakespeare may well have shaped his thought, for this passage (*Essays*, p.316; from "Poetry and Tradition," 1907, in *C of A*) is prefaced by the examples of Timon and Cleopatra, and is followed by the observation that any poet "could but come to the understanding of himself, to the mastery of unlocking words after long frequenting of the great Masters."

47. The first two of these quotations are from "The Gyres"; the third from "The Three Bushes"; the last from "The Municipal Gallery Revisited." All are in *Last Poems*, 1940.

48. "Lapis Lazuli," from *Last Poems*, 1940, from which the next two quotations are also drawn. Compare, in "Poetry and Tradition," 1907 (from *C of A*, p.314 in *Essays*): "Shakespeare's persons, when the last darkness has gathered about them, speak out of an ecstasy that is one half the self-surrender of sorrow, and one half the last playing and mockery of the victorious sword, before the defeated world."

49. Compare Sidney's *Defense of Poesie*: "give right honor to the heavenly maker of that maker. . . ." In poetry, "with the force of a divine breath he bringeth things forth far surpassing her [Nature's] doings . . ." "our erected wit maketh us know what perfection is." Or from Scaliger's *Poetice*: "But the poet makes another nature and . . . makes himself another God, as it were. . . . Poetry . . . seems not to narrate the events, . . . but as a God to produce them." Both quoted from *Literary Criticism: Plato to Dryden*, pp.413–14, ed. by Allan H. Gilbert, 1940, American Book Company.

50. "Two Songs from a Play [*The Resurrection*]," Number II, in *The Tower*, 1928.

51. See in *Collected Poems*, pp.102, 103, 105–06, 115, (117–20), 146, 206, 234; and in *Last Poems*, pp.37, 50, 75, 80, 91. Compare also

Housman's theory in *The Name and Nature of Poetry*: the irritation of a grain of sand causes the oyster to produce a pearl. So
with the poet.

52. *Letters to Dorothy Wellesley*, p.135, Oxford University Press,
1940. Dated Jan. 28, 1937.

53. "Meditations in Times of Civil War," in *The Tower*, 1928.

54. In Yeats's philosophical system, the poet striving to create ideal
beauty in his poetry is the Will yearning toward the Mask, its
antithesis, and also the Creative Mind reshaping its opposed Body
of Fate: "By the help of an image I call to my own opposite,
summon all That I have handled least, least looked upon." "Art
is but a vision of reality." These quotations are from "Ego
Dominus Tuus," in *The Wild Swans at Coole*. The poem should
be read entire, since Yeats analyzes in detail the sources of Dante's
and of Keats's creative energies. Like so many of his poems, this
is a dialogue, between "Hic" and "Ille." Here is what he says of
Keats:

Hic.   No one denies to Keats love of the world;
       Remember his deliberate happiness.
Ille.   His art is happy, but who knows his mind?
       I see a schoolboy when I think of him,
       With face and nose pressed to a sweet-shop window,
       For certainly he sank into his grave
       His senses and his heart unsatisfied,
       And made—being poor, ailing and ignorant,
       Shut out from all the luxury of the world,
       The coarse-bred son of a livery-stable keeper—
       Luxuriant song.

55. *Essays*, p.496. From *Per Amica Silentia Lunae*, 1917.

56. "The Gyres," in *Last Poems*, 1940.

57. "A Nativity," in *Last Poems*, 1940.

58. "Under Ben Bulben," in *Last Poems*, 1940.

59. "Words," in *The Green Helmet*, 1910.

60. "A Woman Homer Sung," in *The Green Helmet*, 1910.

61. *Last Poems*, 1940.

62. Poems may be written as imaginary ideal answers to people who in real life refuse to understand or listen:

> O heart, be at peace, because
> Nor knave nor dolt can break
> What's not for their applause,
> Being for a woman's sake.
> —"Against Unworthy Praise," in
> *The Green Helmet*, 1910.

Compare my analysis of the genesis of a poem by Genevieve Taggard in *Poets at Work*, pp.63–70, ed. by Charles D. Abbott, 1948, Harcourt, Brace; and Auden's essay "Squares and Oblongs" in the same volume, pp.163–81. Auden says: "The ideal audience the poet imagines consists of the beautiful who go to bed with him, the powerful who invite him to dinner and tell him secrets of state, and his fellow-poets. The actual audience . . ." is something quite different.

63. Of this mood of ecstasy, when the poet is "blessed and could bless," Yeats writes that "I seem to understand that I enter upon it the moment I cease to hate. I think the common condition of our life is hatred—I know that this is so with me—irritation with public or private events or persons." Yet Yeats does not find that "love" is the best word to describe the ecstasy, "for we may love unhappily. And plainly, when I have closed a book too stirred to go on reading, and in those brief intense visions of sleep, I have something about me that, though it makes me love, is more like innocence. I am in the place where the daemon is, but I do not think he is with me until I begin to make a new personality, selecting among those images, seeking always to satisfy a hunger. . . ."—*Essays*, pp.533–34. From *Per Amica Silentia Lunae*, 1917.

64. "A Prayer for My Daughter," in *Michael Robartes and the Dancer*, 1921.

65. "The Tower," in *The Tower*, 1928.

66. Quoted from Auden's *Collected Poems*, Random House, 1945. Reprinted by permission of the publishers.

CHAPTER FIVE

1. This possibility is mentioned because it is what I tried to do in a paper called "The Modern Myth of the Modern Myth," published in the *English Institute Essays: 1947*, Columbia University Press, 1948.

2. See *Life and the Dream*, Mary Colum, 1947, Doubleday, New York; *Yeats: The Man and the Masks*, Richard Ellmann, 1948, Macmillan, New York; *Letters on Poetry From W. B. Yeats to Dorothy Wellesley*, 1940, Oxford University Press, N. Y. and London; *J. B. Yeats: Letters to his Son W. B. Yeats and Others, 1869–1922*, 1944, edited by Joseph Hone, Faber and Faber, London; *Scattering Branches*, ed. by Stephen Gwynn, Macmillan, London, 1940; *The Poetry of William Butler Yeats*, Louis MacNeice, 1941, Oxford University Press, New York; *W. B. Yeats, 1865–1939*, Joseph M. Hone, 1942, Macmillan, London. See also the issue of *The Southern Review*, Vol. VII, No. 3, Winter 1941–42, devoted entirely to critical studies of Yeats.

3. "Among School Children," in *The Tower*, 1928.

4. "We should satirise rather than praise. . . . Original virtue arises from the discovery of evil."—*ABs*, p.255. From *T of V*, 1922.

5. Compare "Anashuya and Vijaya," with its note in the *Collected Poems*, 1933, and "The Three Bushes" in *Last Poems*, 1940. Yeats says a great deal about his poems, their purpose and genesis, in his own notes to *Collected Poems*, much of which is paraphrased or quoted direct in this survey. Often these notes were written much later than the original poems. Just as he felt at liberty to change and improve his poems through successive versions, so he accepted the responsibility of glossing passages or themes which his readers had found difficult.

6. "Reconciliation."

7. "The Coming of Wisdom with Time."

8. "To a poet, who would have me praise certain bad poets, imitators of his and mine." See also "The Fascination of What's Difficult."

9. "All Things Can Tempt Me."

10. Joseph Hone's biography of Yeats, 1942, Macmillan, pp.265 ff.
See also William M. Roth's *Catalogue of English and American
First Editions*, 1939, New Haven, p.43.

11. "The Phases of the Moon," "The Double Vision of Michael
Robartes," "Michael Robartes and the Dancer." His phrase is from
his Notes to *Collected Poems*, p.450; the note is dated 1922.

12. *Collected Poems*, Notes, p.450.

13. *A Study of History*, p.217, D. C. Somervell's Abridgement, Oxford University Press, 1947. See *passim*, but particularly pp.209–
30. The seven examples specifically analyzed in this section of
the abridgement of Toynbee come no further than Dante and
Machiavelli. The theory, of course, is illuminating in modern times
as well. It can be applied not only to Yeats, but, for other examples,
to Tolstoi, Henry James, Proust, Eliot, Joyce, Stein, Auden.

14. Compare "Paudeen" in *Responsibilities*, 1914. For this theory
of withdrawal and return, it should be quoted in full:

> Indignant at the fumbling wits, the obscure spite
> Of our old Paudeen in his shop, I stumbled blind
> Among the stones and thorn-trees, under morning light;
> Until a curlew cried and in the luminous wind
> A curlew answered; and suddenly thereupon I thought
> That on the lonely height where all are in God's eye,
> There cannot be, confusion of our sound forgot,
> A single soul that lacks a sweet crystalline cry.

Compare also:

> driven from the populous door,
> He seeks high waters and the mountain birds
> To claim a portion of their solitude.
> > —*The King's Threshold*, 1904.
> > (Quoted from *Collected Plays*,
> > p.142.)

15. "Easter, 1916," "Sixteen Dead Men," "The Rose Tree," "On a
Political Prisoner," and "The Leaders of the Crowd." All in
Michael Robartes and the Dancer.

16. "To a Young Beauty," in *The Wild Swans at Coole*, 1919.

17. *ABs*, p.97. From *Reveries*, 1914. Compare also, p.96: "I did not believe with my intellect that you could be carried away body and soul, but I believed with my emotions and the belief of the country people made that easy."

18. "The Three Bushes," in *Last Poems*, 1940.

19. "Among School Children," in *The Tower*, 1928.

20. "What is a poet? asks Diamond in *At the Back of the North Wind*. The reply is 'A man who is glad of something, and tries to make other people glad of it too.' But the writer, Francis Mac-Donald, puts this cheerful answer into the mouth of Death." From "True Poetry Is Praise," by Helmut Kuhn, *Theology Today*, Vol. IV, No. 2, July 1947, p.254.

21. *Essays*, pp.312 and 314. From "Poetry and Tradition" (1907) in *C of A*.